S0-BQZ-939

Use the Fine China & Drive the Classic

I don't think it's a gender thing. For years, women have accumulated and set aside fine Irish linen, bone china and monogrammed silver as they built their hope chests while we men have cleaned and put away braces of Parker Brothers' shotguns and Garcia fishing gear in anticipation of that future "special day". All too often, it simply doesn't arrive or when it does, the original luster of the event is often dimmed by the diminished energy that results from the delay of doing.

This same "save the best for later" attitude is also afoot with some car collectors. They accumulate and create "trailer queens" that only see pavement under power going from the edge of the trailer ramp to the designated show site. Now, there's no sin in the accumulation of a vast collection but there's probably more real satisfaction by planning for the open road and letting other people catch an up-close glimpse of your mechanical mate.

> "Pleasure, like other simple ideas, cannot be described . . . the way of knowing is . . . only by experience."
>
> —LOCKE—

The accomplished collectors we know, such as Corky Coker, president of Coker Tire, agrees with the "Get Out The Classic" movement. Coker, for example, has launched a new campaign and namesake award to help boost awareness of America's driving heritage by urging owners and enthusiasts to get their rides out of the garage and back on the road. For example, Coker Tire is encouraging major car collections and auto museums to open their collections free of charge to those who arrive in their own classic car. Corky takes his mission personally, "We want to practice what we preach," he notes. "You can't get the smiles unless you do the miles." I personally hope the magic of the movement catches on.

It's fitting to close with an encouragement for you to begin to experience and enjoy the pleasure that can be realized by driving the automobiles that constitute your collection, whether it numbers one or one hundred. Lewis Grizzard provides the perfect motoring mantra from his stint as Grand Marshal of the TransSouth 500 when he bypassed the traditional call to post of "Gentlemen, start your engines," when with his unique Southern flair said, "Gentlemen, y'all can crank 'em up."

So, don't wait too long. Crank 'em up now, get 'em on the road and share the joy associated with driving fine old cars. If nothing else, look at it as a way of protecting your investment.

Drive in Peace,

Gerry Durnell

Gerry Durnell
Editor & Publisher

1

Automobile Quarterly

The Connoisseur's Publication of Motoring
– Today, Yesterday, and Tomorrow –

GERRY DURNELL
Editor & Publisher

KAYE BOWLES-DURNELL
Associate Publisher

JOHN C. DURNELL
Chief Operations Officer, Technical Editor

TRACY POWELL
Managing Editor

JOHN EVANS
Chief Financial Officer

DAN BULLEIT
Art Director

ROD HOTTLE
Administrative Assistant

L. SCOTT BAILEY
Founding Editor and Publisher

Contributing Photographers
PHIL SCALIA

Contributing Writers
SIMON MOORE
MICHAEL L. BROMLEY
TRACY POWELL
LEIGH DORINGTON
KARL LUDVIGSEN
BROOKS T. BRIERLEY
GRIFFITH BORGESON

www.autoquarterly.com

ISBN 1-59613-051-2
(978-1-59613-051-7)

Printed in Korea

Contents

VOLUME 46, NUMBER 3 • THIRD QUARTER 2006

Cover: "Brothers of Destiny" watercolor

Left: "Moal Special" 24 x 36 inches, watercolor

3

A Missing
Alfa Romeo
Monza
Comes Back to Life
An International Search and Rescue Story

W hen fresh from Alfa Romeo's Portello works in 1933, this Monza competed in Grand Prix and major sports car events throughout Europe including the famous Mille Miglia. After its active international career, it raced in local events in Switzerland before being crashed and broken up in the 1940s. The main mechanical parts went to England and the frame was chopped to make a farm cart. There are many wonderful stories about re-uniting the major components of old cars that have been broken up but this is one of the strangest. Let's start by briefly describing the 8C2300 Alfa Romeo and then go into this particular car's fascinating history.

BY SIMON MOORE   PHOTOGRAPHY BY PHIL SCALIA

BACKGROUND TO THE 8C2300 ALFA ROMEO

Following the success of the Vittorio Jano designed P2 Grand Prix cars in 1924-25, with which they won the "world championship" of the time, Alfa Romeo concentrated on road-going sports cars with Jano designing a series of six cylinder engined cars with either single or twin overhead camshafts, some of which were also supercharged. These blown 6C1500 and 6C1750 (after the cubic capacity) were very successful in sports car competition, for example winning the Mille Miglia for three years in a row, 1928-29-30, the Spa 24-hours, the TT in Northern Ireland and so on.

For 1931 Jano designed a new car, still with a simple frame, semi-elliptic springs front and back and rod-operated brakes but fitted with a straight eight supercharged engine with the same cylinder dimensions as the 6C1750. This was the 8C2300 – produced in short or long chassis configuration plus an ultra-short pure racing "Monza" pointed tail form – and which won the Mille Miglia four times (1932-33-34), Le Mans four times (1931 through 1934), the

Above: The entry list for the 1935 Bergamo GP had Soffietti driving a Maserati, with car no. 8, but it is clearly a Monza. The only one in Swiss colors that year was 2211136. The hairpin must have been acute, judging by the angle of those front wheels. Below: Ruesch and Maag on the left had caught up with Battaglia in 2111043 by the time they reached Roma in the 1934 Mille Miglia, despite starting four minutes later.

1931 Italian GP, the 1932 Monaco GP and many more events, both in the hands of the works team, Scuderia Ferrari and private owners.

EARLY HISTORY OF CHASSIS NUMBER 2211136

The Alfa Romeo factory decided to close down their works racing team at the end of 1932 after a tremendously successful year racing, primarily, the Tipo B "monoposto" in Grand Prix events. They built up a number of new Monzas for sale over the following winter so that both private entrants and small teams could compete in both sports car events and Grand Prix in 1933. While probably the most important private team was the Scuderia Ferrari (who had drivers like Tazio Nuvolari on their books), Louis Chiron and Rudi Caracciola teamed

up to form Scuderia CC while other drivers ran solo. Although we cannot be 100-percent certain who owned 2211136 in 1933, it is likely, by a process of elimination, that it was the car driven in some Grand Prix events by talented Algerian Guy Moll whose results so impressed Enzo Ferrari that he went on to race for Scuderia Ferrari before being killed in a Tipo B at Pescara in 1934.

At the beginning of 1934, 2211136 moved to Switzerland and was raced by Hans Ruesch and Ulrich Maag in the Swiss racing colours of red and white. However, the car was not officially imported into Switzerland at that time, nor did it race there. It was either run on Swiss dealer plates or on Napoli ones — Ruesch had a house there and registered other cars in that city.

Ruesch and Maag ran the 1934 Mille Miglia in the car, fitted with cycle fenders, but failed to finish. Maag then ran in two events at the Nurburgring finishing 6th

Eugen Bjornstad converted his ex-works Monza in Sweden to single-seater form, using twin rear wheels with huge spikes in the tires for racing on ice and snow. This is the original body now fitted to Bill Binnie's car.

Ruesch and Maag pressing on through mountainous countryside in the 1934 Mille Miglia.

in the Eifelrennen but failing to finish in the German GP. Tragically, he was killed in a road accident on his way to compete in the car (with Ruesch) in the Targa Abruzzo at Pescara in August that year.

The car was becoming a little old and therefore marginally competitive by 1935. But Ruesch, with co-driver Guatta, finished an excellent 4th in the Mille Miglia. He also finished 8th in the Targa Florio in Sicily and 3rd in the sports car class in the Kesselberg hill climb. In addition, Soffietti finished 4th at the only GP run in Bergamo, borrowing the car for the occasion. After that season, the car was officially imported into Switzerland in October and sold to Emilio Rampinelli. He ran some minor events before selling it on and the car descended into obscurity being subsequently owned by Hans Taveri and Paul Waldner. Finally, the car was apparently involved in an accident around late 1947 or early 1948 while owned by Arthur Hueberger, a garage owner from Goldach in the North East part of Switzerland, after which it was broken up.

Slowly, bits and pieces were recovered in the search for the missing essentials for a complete restoration build-out. The chassis frame (above) from 2211136, once used as a hay cart, and the frame pieces as discovered (below).

numbers of those other bits that were numbered by the factory (gearbox, back axle) purchased by Lord Ridley indicate that there was a very good chance that they all came from the same car, except the earlier steering box number, which also has a 3x33 ratio, more normal in a road car than a Monza. Lord Ridley modified the 6C1750, fitting the 8C steering box and the bigger engine and used the car in that form. The cross member on which the front engine mounts sits is an 8C piece not a 6C one – which may or may not have come with the engine from Bartlett.

The UK log book for 101014852 shows the change of engine recorded on Aug. 25, 1954, so it took Ridley a bit over a year to effect the changes. Subsequently, following Lord Ridley's death in 1967, the car was owned by A.A. Morse, and Julian Calvert before passing to Gerald Batt in the South of England in 1978. He decided to discard the Castagna body and have a replica 8C2300 Le Mans Touring body made by Dick Brockman. The new coachwork was based

THE ENGINE

In the November 1952 issue of *Motor Sport*, London Alfa dealer Jack Bartlett advertised an 8C2300 engine, gearbox and back axle spares for sale. How Bartlett had acquired this collection is unknown but maybe he was approached by the vendor since he was always advertising Alfas and was well known through his regular advertisements in the specialist press. This collection was purchased by Lord Ridley who owned several other pre-war Alfa Romeos including a long chassis 8C2300 (2311243) and two 8C2900s, one open (412022) and one closed (412024). He also owned a Castagna-bodied 6C1750 (chassis number 101014852) that he had bought from a Mr. Montgomery of London in 1951 - and had decided to modify the car by fitting a more powerful eight cylinder motor, hence his purchase of the 8C engine, gearbox and differential from Bartlett.

The engine number was 2211136 and the part

The gorgeous, sweeping lines and seductive angles of the Tipo 8C came together again after an extensive search and an immaculate restoration.

on inspection of the very original ex Mike Hawthorn car, chassis number 2311202 but the result was not exactly correct in all details.

In late 1998, the car passed via a Christies auction to William Binnie in New Hampshire who sent the car to Dave George's restoration shop outside Philadelphia for some work. The 8C parts were removed from the car and placed to one side while a spare engine was acquired from Murray Rainey in England and that, together with some other spares, was used to get the car as purchased back together for onward sale. Up to this point, there is essentially nothing new compared to my knowledge when I wrote my three volume book "The Legendary 2.3". However, Bill Binnie then initiated some detective work and the subsequent story, however far-fetched it seems, is definitely worth recording.

THE CHASSIS

The start point was to see if any of Jack Bartlett's records survived. The author was aware that the records of his trading in 1934-35 had survived but thought that the later ones had been destroyed after he died in the South of France in the 1970s. Research confirmed that indeed the records from 1934 and 1935 survive, but nothing else. So where to turn to now? Strangely, the answer came from down the road from Dave George's Pennsylvania shop.

In the 1960s and 1970s, the late Rob de la Rive ("Robbie") Box was working in the old car trade in Switzerland, initially for Erwin Eckert and then for himself. Robbie scoured Switzerland for old cars and even ventured into the Eastern Bloc (as it then was) looking for treasures in barns, lock-ups and garages. The market was not that developed in those days and there were few buyers around so many of the wonderful cars that he uncovered, especially Bugattis,

Every detail was addressed in the rebuild of 2211136

14

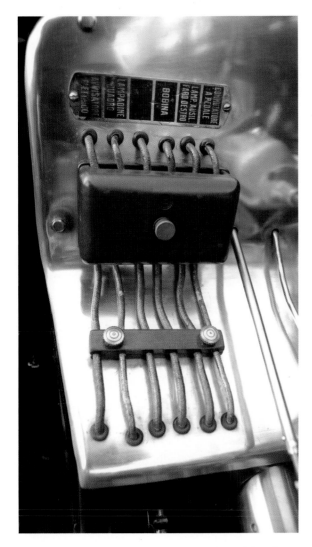

The authenticity of the body was verified beyond doubt when the driver's side piece was cleaned clearly showing the proper stamping.

ended up in Mulhouse with the Schlumpf brothers. Robbie became a good friend and helped with my research into Alfa Romeos in later years.

One of the other active dealers in Europe at that time was the late Bart Loyens in Hamm in the country of Luxembourg. After his death, all his records and correspondence ended up being purchased by Philadelphia neuro surgeon and car collector, Dr. Fred Simeone and it was there that the first signs of the chassis frame from 2211136 emerged from Bart's correspondence. A gentleman named Franz Erni advertised the frame for sale in a local Swiss newspaper in early 1978 and Loyens followed it up. Initially a price of Swiss Francs 400 was agreed but then Loyens thought better of it and cancelled the deal. This frame had been used as a hay cart and was missing its engine, gearbox, rear axle and one chassis cross member. "Was it really an 8C frame?" you may ask. Well, many years ago, I heard the same story from Robbie Box who had followed up the approach to Loyens, visited the location (near Goldach) and said that it was definitely Alfa. I trust Robbie's judgement since that was his business but there is always a slight chance that he was wrong. The only photo to survive (on page 8) is really too fuzzy to be certain but it is clearly missing the cross member on which the engine mounts – which was an 8C piece that Ridley used in modifying the 6C.

In those days, there was no real market for such a frame so the whole thing was forgotten until Bill Binnie came along. After several months of trying, he traced Franz Erni who had worked on river barges all his life and was seldom at home! Bill visited him in June 2000 and found out more information. He had bought the "hay cart" from a farmer near Weingarten named Carl Kuhn who had used it for several years. Once the deal with Loyens fell apart, Erni stored the frame in his father's barn and basically forgot about it. His mother died in 1986 and his father made some changes to the family home when Franz's sister moved in to take care of their father. Some things were sent for scrap, seemingly including the hay cart. Despite much searching in the area, Bill Binnie found no trace of the frame including searching the nearest scrap yard, Muller's. It seems that this scrap yard did actually recycle scrap (as against accumulate scrap like many yards) and the hay cart has gone forever.

Bill also went to Carl Kuhn's farm which was remarkably untouched and original, if disorganized! Unfortunately Carl had died in 1997, and, while there were lots of car parts lying around, there was nothing obviously Alfa Romeo.

Not to be deterred, Bill set about looking into what scrap yards service that area of Switzerland. The Swiss rarely throw anything away and the scrap yards often keep parts for many years. This is also evident from the fact that Gondrand, a big trucking company still active today (their big yellow trucks can be seen all over Europe's highways) still have their early 1930s records listing chassis numbers of Monza Alfas moved under carnets. As the Americans say, he hit "pay dirt" in 2001 at Truringer's yard half way between the Kuhn farm and Goldach where the last owner of the complete car had lived.

Amongst a load of "junk" in a very dark shed, as well as Bugatti and Alfa Romeo parts, Bill and Dave found the rear pieces of the chassis frame, cut off when the hay cart was made, maybe 4 feet long. Mindful of my criticism of people who fail to have "as found" photos, they took photos then and there which you can see here. Better still, amazingly, the driver's side piece was cleaned and showed clearly "2211136" stamped there. So the frame of the car today is based on those rear sections plus newly made steel. An unscrupulous person might have claimed to have found the complete frame but it adds to the credibility of the story that only a part was found and photographed.

THE BODY

Obviously, the original body had really been scrapped years ago so the story moves to Copenhagen in Denmark where ex-works Monza 2111041 has lived for many years. This car had a hard life, being raced by the factory throughout

1932 before being actively campaigned by Norwegian driver Eugen Bjornstad over several seasons including coming to the United States for the 1936 Vanderbilt Cup. After the war, it was raced with a V8 Ford engine before arriving in Denmark with a sympathetic owner. In my book, I recorded that owner Svend Hauberg had a new body made and was nearing the completion of the restoration.

Bill and Dave contacted Hauberg and, following some negotiations, the original body off 2111041 was sold to be fitted to 2211136. Some work was required since the body had been narrowed to single seat configuration before World War II.

THE COMPLETE CAR

So what does Bill have? He has all the mortal remains of the original chassis frame with the missing part reconstructed. Judging from the part numbers, he has the engine, gearbox and back axle and some other components from 2211136, re-fitted to the frame. He also has an original 1932 Alfa Romeo Monza body, brought back to two-seater form. A number of other genuine original 8C2300 parts are also fitted especially the steering box and column. To make the car usable in events like the Mille Miglia, Dave has fitted wings and a full-width screen the Hauberg body had never had these fitted, being an out-and-out racer. In fact, the car ran faultlessly in the 2002 event round Italy from Brescia to Roma and back.

Overall, the car today represents a far more complete Monza than could have been dreamt of when the Ridley car with a 6C chassis was auctioned in 1998 and I am most impressed with Bill Binnie's dogged "never give up" research that eventually enabled Dave George to complete the final car that you see on these pages. AQ

Bill Binnie can stand proudly alongside his resurrected Alfa.

Motoring Through Tough Times:
The Nineteen Seventies

The 1970s and automobiles. Seventies and cars.

S*ay it a few times. The words neither rhyme nor seem a happy fit. That evocative image of a car that defines an age goes missing there — or worse, it's filled by Gremlins and other ghosts of what should not have been. Enthusiasm is little drawn by that most exceptional car of the decade, the Honda Civic with the CVCC engine, especially since its remarkable ascent marked the decay of so much else around it. And of the period's truly great machines, of the shockingly good-for-its-price Datsun 240Z, of the accessible and fast BMW 2002tii and the 5- and 7-Series, of the Mercedes-Benz S-Class with its monstrous, oil crisis-defying 450 SEL 6.9, and of the Supercars, the M1, Pantera, Esprit, 911 Turbo and Countach — they all seem out of place in their own time.*

BY MICHEAL L, BROMLEY

First, a couple myths. The small car was not a creation of the Energy Crisis. And there never was a shortage of petroleum. As ever with the products of turmoil, both these dominant associations with the 1970s arose partly from the laws of unintended consequence, partly from hyperventilated reaction to them, partly from reality, and mostly from general foolishness. Oh, and one more: Jimmy Carter didn't invent the "double nickel." Nixon did, having settled on it after trying for five-oh first.

SMALL, AND GETTING BIGGER AT IT ALL THE TIME

A principal reason the U.S. industry did not entirely collapse in the 1970s was because it had already collapsed long before. The "Big Four," more appropriately the "Big Three-1/2," of GM, Ford, Chrysler and American Motors, represented consolidation and death of the old independents that well before succumbed to either economic disruption, wage and price controls, collective bargaining, or the mass scales that allowed their larger competitors to soak up those conditions and spit out profits and cars. In 1969, a low-level burn of imports accounted for just under 12 percent of the market, with most of it coming from a certain company in Germany. By 1980, imports held double that share, now overwhelmingly from Japan. Somehow, the success of this new and vigorous competition is seen as the fault of the Indigenous Four, that they ought to have remained enthroned with monopolistic dominion, withstanding all rivals and forever. Somehow, the independents of old were unnatural, ill-equipped rivals, evolutionary rejects in the natural order of the American automobile.

Whatever a normal market is supposed to be, Detroit's domination was not satisfactory to the American consumer. When Detroit let itself—or was allowed to be—Detroit, it made really good cars that people wanted throughout the 1970s. But those cars didn't define the period, and they didn't fulfill the new needs. Not even the VW "bug" made it far into the decade. Cars would have to be different now, and meet previously unthinkable demands of a new regulatory state. American cars ended the decade as products with too many demands and intentions. And as Detroit shrunk, the import competition became more American, in design, in style, annual makeover,

Pictured here during the 1976 presidential campaign, Jimmy Carter greets folks down-home style at brother Billy's gas station.

amenities, and, ultimately, in fabrication. To keep up with it, Detroit had to re-learn quality and value, perhaps an ongoing struggle.

In 1974 an industry observer noted, "The Big Three auto companies are being dragged, kicking and screaming into the 1970s." The first evidence was that as 1973 oil shortages loomed the only 4-cylinder domestics were the "sub-compacts" Pinto and Vega. The Pinto's engine was from Europe, and the Vega's, potentially great but sadly not, was at best problematic. The rest of the American small car field sold sixes and optional eights. With the oil squeeze consumers paid premiums for anything with fewer than eight cylinders. Whoever had inventory in small, used or new, sold cars. Detroit scrambled to convert from Impalas and Furys to Novas and Valiants. Having re-positioned itself as a small car maker well before the oil embargo, AMC started looking downright brilliant.

Expecting the worst, Washington policy-makers prepared for wartime-like ration cards not seen since the deepest of WWII.

GM had attempted a genuine rediscovery in the Vega project with new production techniques using robots, low parts count, OHV aluminum engine, front disks, and a new labor policy. But compromise dominated results, not innovation.

Like its mentor the Model T, the VW legend came of its enduring sameness. Since a '70 looked like a '65, the cars kept their value. This feature was sweetness itself to the anti-corporatism of the era, and was why the car skated so long on obsolescence. In fixating on and entirely misreading the Volkswagen business model, the American car industry condemned itself to something that was impossible to replicate and already dated. Thus Detroit's attempts at re-invention became half-starts and half-attempts to get through market upheavals and changing conditions that seemed always a step ahead. Facing government, intellectual, and consumer animosity, Detroit became unsure. Its sense of identity disrupted by the Volkswagen's success, it didn't know itself any more.

In the late 1950s Detroit faced a similar crisis. The wild success of the "compact" Rambler and the growth of imports—one report counted 81 lines sold—frightened the Big Three into radical change. Going from the '59 models to the '60s saw GM nearly turn over itself from the Cadillac to the Corvair. A sudden sobriety of design followed. Aftermarket suppliers sold de-chrome and fin-removal kits. The Big Three reply to the small car was vigorous. With the Corvair and the Pontiac Tempest, GM demonstrated a flair beyond the wildest fins that 1959 otherwise means to the popular mind of today. The cars and their engines were innovative and purposeful. Then came Ford with the Falcon, Plymouth with the Valiant, and GM's own 4-cylinder follow-up, the Chevy II. The cars showed taste, attention to the customer, and innovation. And it worked. Ramblers sales dropped, and imports fell by almost half.

Meanwhile, popular culture sorted out the meaning of the small car. Advice columns taught how to drive them and states worried about lost tax revenue. The small car was at once a relief to air pollution and a menace to safety. And the shrinks, of course, came

While GM scrambled for smaller engines and a smaller small car, the next AMC was built to "cut across segments," AMC's Roy Chapin, Jr. said. "It's not a car about which you can say that's a sub-compact, that's a compact, that's a sports car or that's a whatever. It's a car that we think is going to have almost universal appeal for some people." That car, the Pacer, arrived along with the Chevette, the latest of Detroit's "next Model T." Chasing the chimera of the "universal" car, Detroit once again fooled itself into trying to be what it was not. The Chevette, at least, was a true small car, with a 4-speed, 1.4-liter engine, and 40 mpg performance. The Pacer came in heavy, overpriced, with two too many cylinders, and rather than cutting across segments it became a segment of its own. Then, with the fuel crunch eased, the new word in Detroit was "flexibility." The 4-cylinder Mustang II arrived as a "luxury compact" and offered an optional six. The next year there was an eight.

SMALL ALL OVER AGAIN

In response to the seemingly unstoppable VW, the 1969-70 Ford Maverick and AMC Hornet announced the revival of the American small car, and were soon followed by the Pinto, Gremlin and Vega, all aimed at the bug. Motorsports journalist John Radosta recognized the flaws in them that would come to define the American small car. In the Vega he complained of its sluggishness, the "excessively long 'throw'" of the shifter, the "sterile ... ugly" trim, and the sloppy design. Of the Hornet, he wrote that "no one should have put up with shoddy workmanship..." Of the Pinto, "its ideal milieu is city and suburb, and not much beyond." Overall, it was "disappointing." Radosta understood that the American small car was making for itself a bad reputation, that it needed more than just a spec-sheet resemblance to the competition.

up with the subconscious craving for the compact car derived of "a feeling of guilt about American ostentatiousness." And no sooner than popular culture digested this strange new automotive identity than Detroit dropped it. The Tempest gave up its four cylinders and "transaxle" rear transmission, which had allowed for no "hump" and shorter overall length. All pretense of looking like a small, front-wheel-drive European car was out. Out came the Mustang, a "sporty" upgrade

would lure temporarily economy-minded customers into what they really wanted in luxuries and add-ons. Of the 1959-61 innovations, only the Chevy II, with its 4-cylinders, and the Corvair remained outside ordinary design. And the VW kept selling. And Detroit kept obsessing over it. In going after the beetle Detroit followed a misplaced definition of a value car. By the time the new American beetle-killers were out, the aura was off the bug, and a new threat had emerged.

and, for a moderate $2,300, fully automatic transmission, seemed not a threat to anyone in particular. Stylistically more like a Fiat, technologically simple, the car had no market definition, except this: it was reliable, buyers liked it, and it got better every year. Toyota had carefully studied the American market and concluded that flexibility was prized by American buyers as much as economy and quality. The Japanese cars were sent with American-style *à-la-carte* choices, which served the dual purpose of meeting consumer demands and making happy dealers. Also offering the economy Corolla and high-end Crown models, Toyota operated a scale model of Alfred Sloan's 1920s General Motors. And with the geographic accident of California their largest market, Japanese makers benefitted from early exposure to the state's emissions rules and demanding consumers. The learning came early and relatively pain free, and taught crucial lessons in operating in the American market. Above all, the Japanese entry was perfectly timed for Detroit's attack on the beetle. For U.S. makers it seemed an easy repeat of 1959: just slap the problem onto engineering, throw it over to marketing, and the dealers would move 'em out. Then once the consumer got over the fever, grow the cars to a more profitable size. The success of the sixties taught Detroit all wrong.

A familiar scene in the '70s: long lines at the gas pump.

of the Falcon Futura, the Pontiac GTO, born of dropping a 389 into a Tempest, and the new Chevy "sports compact car," the Camaro. The car culture exploded along with horsepower and the rise of the Boomers. Unfortunately, not all the lessons and rewards lined up. Detroit arrogance was reinforced, and the idea stuck that simply cutting wheelbase and engine size

The first Japanese cars to hit America were oddities. Settling first in the West Coast, they built their reputation little by little. And little by little Americans came to know them, and little by little sales grew and grew, so much so that in 1968 Toyota launched the first of 15 transport ships the company had commissioned. The 1968 Corona, with its 90 hp engine,

RALPH

Before there was "auto safety," there was "highway safety," a movement formally marked by the 1909 creation of the "National Highway Protective Society." With the death that accompanies the automobile, every generation finds original urgency to the problem, rediscovering old and unfinished solutions that are then mixed into the peculiarities of the new day. The movement that culminated in the 1970s federal regulatory regime came of the usual dread at the roadway destruction combined with the nationalized solutions of post-New Deal public policy. The building of the Interstate Highway System gave

In 1975, Ford and GM tried to match the cars people wanted with what the government thought they should buy. Luxury car owners were surveyed, and the result was a "vehement" reaction against the suggestion that luxury cars were "disgraceful" and should be banned. The 1976 Ford Thunderbird is one of the examples of giving this group what they wanted.

new life to the safety movement as well as rhetorical opportunity for demands that something must be done. As a journalist observed of a safety conference in the 1950s, "The officials were uniformly opposed to accidents and traffic deaths...." The peculiarities at work in the 1960s were the period's anti-establishment individualism, environmentalism and loathing of all things corporate, which joined to hijack the latest safety craze in the name of "the consumer." An attempted *coup d'état* of Detroit by an operation

known today as Ralph Nader, Inc. did not succeed, although its leader was empowered by Detroit arrogance, especially over at the infamous "14th Floor" of the GM headquarters. The movement culminated in the National Traffic and Motor Vehicle Safety Act of 1966 and a series of other laws that led to regulation of the automobile "from bumper to bumper."

Nader was a uniquely effective self-promoter just awaiting his moment. His 1959 article, "The Safe Car You Can't Buy" had found no audience. Six years later

and amidst revolt against standing order, America was rather disposed to hear that its automobile industry had betrayed the people. While Nader neither created nor owned the safety movement, he would become its face and the principal force for turning it into a national fetish. The summer before Nader's "Unsafe at Any Speed" was released, and when he was just another obscure D.C. activist, some of his most earnest allies, the trial attorneys, gathered at the Fontainebleau Hotel in Miami Beach. A 1956 theory called "the crashworthiness doctrine" was just then finding its way into the courts. It held automakers responsible for the "second collision" after a crash, that is to say, all injuries. At this convention of self-

If anything of the 1960s was counter-culture, it was the rear-engined Corvair, only it ended up as a counter-counter-culture, a target and victim of the anti-corporate 1960s activism.

incident involving one fell to legal scrutiny, no matter the cause. The next revolution came in the discovery by the trial lawyers of the quickest way to the deepest pocket, the class action suit. In 1969, GM was sued on

qualities." That Cadillac fins killed children is alien to us today. That Detroit was more interested in profits through marketing gimmicks was the primary justification for the radical safety movement. Early 1960s Kennedy optimism would turn downright gloomy as the idea that every aspect of the economy could and should be tamed by the regulatory and courtroom leash, especially Detroit's profits. For the extreme safety activists, the word "profit" became *prima facie* proof of negligence.

SAFE AND CLEAN AT ALL COSTS

Such a difference between 1956, when Ford offered optional seatbelts, and 1967, when the entire industry sat on its hands before putting in three-point "harness" belts without a government order. It is far from clear that the industry would not have adopted the harnesses without government edict. It is very clear that the industry had learned to use Washington for cover. All American makers issued seatbelts as standard equipment for the '64 model year. Perhaps it should have come before then. But the government safety regime proved no better at getting citizens to buckle up than the industry had. In 1956, a private research group rather accurately predicted that, if commonly used, seatbelts would save 19,000 lives a year. By 1969, and three years into federal mandates, more Americans were dying on the road than ever. Then, in 1974 the government managed to turn a good many Americans *against* seatbelts. Frustrated that motorists didn't just stop killing each other, especially since the bureaucracy was under attack for making cars more expensive while the road carnage continued apace, the government demanded some kind of "passive restraint" system in all front seats. GM alone had a viable airbag, but like the others, GM worried that the technology was too costly for general use. The solution was the "interlocking device" that would prevent the engine

described "legal entrepreneurs," lawyer Harry Philo told the gathered about "a drawing board error in the basic rear suspension geometry" of the Chevrolet Corvair, that had opened the way for 160 lawsuits against GM. Philo further instructed the lawyers how to turn a simple driver negligence suit into a "major" case, and he predicted 5,000 such lawsuits the next year alone. The manufacturers were adding new safety features to the 1966 lines, he said, so they ought to be liable for the negligence in not having had those items before. Following Nader's book, Corvair lawsuits turned into a national parade. Every incident or near

behalf of an undetermined hundreds of thousands of truck owners who knew nothing of the case.

Where Philo's and Nader's strategies conjoined came in the use of the profit motive to prove corporate malfeasance. The idea that business was more concerned with money than the public good was as old as demagogy itself. Even with autos, it wasn't Nader's invention. A typical expression from 1960 went that "children will continue to be injured or killed in driveways because the driver's view of them is blocked by functionless fins or high hoods and by windshields designed for esthetic rather than optical from starting if front seat belts were unfastened. The consumer response was hardly "passive." By direct act of Congress, the mandate was rescinded for the next model year.

Another regulation-induced craze was the recall. Post-manufacture fixes weren't new, although the automakers preferred to address problems quietly. After the Bureau of Safety gave in to newspaper pressure to release defect data, every little problem went on the public record. An example: in 1966 Chevrolet called in 1.5 million cars equipped with power-glide

number by market share, the recall label stuck to Detroit and not to Europe or Japan. For Detroit it was a public relations disaster, and all the benefits of the program cannot mitigate that it led to hyper-sensitivity and hyper-conservatism on the part of U.S. automakers who learned to choose inferior but proven designs over better but fresh ones. The recall proved itself no healthy source of innovation.

Moderating behavior and roads saves lives far and away more than automobile design. Modern NHTSA interpretations show that from 1966 to 1978 the num-

more Corvairs, no more GTOs, and instead brought Vegas and Pintos, and other productions whose dangers were born of timidity, not daring.

With the safety and environmental movements headlong into 1970, anti-automobilism had never been so strong since the early 1900s when autos were infernal machines of noise and smoke for exclusive use of the rich to better trample the poor. There are ever momentary seizures of anti-automobile hysteria, but the true automotive paralysis during two mass wars had reminded Americans of how much they loved their cars. Now came the first serious calls for banning automobiles during peacetime since the first of the Motor Age.

In 1969, the California Senate passed a law to outlaw use of gasoline-powered cars in the state by 1975. In August 1970, Senator Gaylord Nelson of Wisconsin, founder of "Earth Day," submitted an amendment to "prohibit the sale of any automobile with an internal combustion engine" as of 1975. Detroit, he said, instead of developing an "alternative engine" wasted $3-5 billion annually on "fashion, frills and fins." Nelson's Earth Day empowered the lunatic edges of the environmentalist movement, with protests against the automobile a dominant theme, and dragging otherwise sane politicians down with it. A few days before the 1970 New York Automobile Show, politicians gathered for a press conference in support of protesters who had been picketing the General Motors building. One of the politicos, the Nassau County executive, and a candidate for governor, said, "The car is not worth our air and our lives and our children's lives. We are here to say 'no' to General Motors and to Ford and to Chrysler. We are here to protest their auto show and to protest their irresponsible abuse of the American public." After concluding in agreement with the proposed ban of the internal-combustion engine, he returned to the limousine that awaited him outside, motor running. He had planned on showing up in a non-polluting, propane car that, it was explained, wasn't available in time.

American Motors' runaway success in the 1967 Rambler "compact" turned Detroit upside-down as the Big Three responded with their own small cars. The Detroit adoption of the compact car legitimized it. Here, the Ford Escort.

transmissions to fix a problem that had occurred five times, each during a snowstorm and none resulting in injury. When questioned as to why the company hadn't anticipated the problem, a spokesman replied that tests on the proving grounds "didn't happen to run into that kind of snow out there." After a decade of recalls totaling 71.5 million domestic and 14.1 million imports from 1966 to 1979, roughly a balanced

ber of lives saved by "vehicle safety technologies" amounted to all of 4,000 people. The horrible waste of the Nader years comes of its single-minded focus on the manufacturer and manufacturer profits while letting the human factor slide through blameless, victimized even, for driving stupid, drunk, tired, or in unsafe weather. The notion that automobiles should be inherently "safe" became a danger unto itself. It meant no

As the regulatory state sharpened its knives, the government and the industry turned their new marriage into a love-hate affair. Detroit resisted where it could and took advantage of every leverage possible, especially as regards the competition. A standard issued in 1970, for example, for raised, 5-mph safety bumpers on 1973 models conveniently followed the panic in Detroit over Volkswagen sales. The overall cost of the 1970s regulatory regime came of the non-competitive nature of central control. The regulations discounted economic responsibility and reward, and favored complacency and dependency, something known as "rent seeking." And the cost was born more heavily by the two smallest makers, who, no mistake, were bankrupt by the end of the decade. By 1978 GM made 60 percent of domestic passenger cars and Ford a quarter. A government study that year concluded that "regulatory requirements" had pushed Chrysler and American Motors to their financial limits. "Even a minor recession" would be "catastrophic." The next year's manufactured oil crisis made the warning more than poignant.

A Perfect Storm

The 1973 oil crisis is usually attributed to the Arab oil embargo. It worsened, but did not cause an ongoing "energy crisis" that started in late 1972. As ever, it was not of a simple cause. A first problem was the Nixon economic program that was at best schizophrenic. He professed belief in the free market and imposed the most severe economic controls since World War II. His 1971 "Wage-Price-Rent Freeze" aimed to limit inflation through a series of voluntary and mandatory wage, price and profits limits that amounted to a national costs-plus system. When controls were relinquished, prices shot upward, which brought back mandatory controls, which brought back shortages.

Another pressure system came from President Eisenhower's import quotas that were to protect America from international oil disruptions. Coupled with Nixon's domestic price controls, the import limits

isolated American oil production from international pricing. The domestic suppliers, of course, were all for it. Meanwhile, the Texas oil fields grew old. The next complication came in refining capacity. Here environmentalism, 1960s social enlightenment, national economic policy, corporate greed, and a spate of tanker spills fell in line, and, as the chairman of the yet powerful Texas Railroad Commission noted, "this country

Ford's tiny Fiesta, 1979.

no longer has the capacity to refine its own petroleum needs." Not a single new refinery had been built since 1958. A heating oil shortage hit during the winter of 1972. When oil quotas were relaxed to relieve the strain, it was, as the director of the Office of Emergency Preparedness noted, "too damned late." The situation was further complicated by varied supply allocations across the nation. In April 1973, the Secretary of the Interior warned that Americans had better "take energy

conservation seriously" or face gasoline shortages over the summer. Some states curtailed speed limits that May. Well before the oil embargo Americans knew gas lines and closed stations. A June survey by the AAA found that 1 percent of the nations' gas stations were closed, 24 percent operated on cut hours, and 7 percent sold rationed quantities.

That, combined with soaring worldwide oil demand, proving the success of the Marshall Plan in the Western Europe economic miracle, the timing couldn't have been better for a little known cartel of oil producing states called OPEC. Newly empowered by nationalized oil fields, and angry at the dollar devaluation Nixon had sparked as part of his anti-inflation program, the oil nations stepped up demands for higher prices and more shares in foreign operations in their countries. It was during this time that the American people were introduced to one Colonel Muammar e-Qaddafi, who was catching on to the fun of geopolitics. Now the various pressure systems converged. On Oct. 6, 1973, Egypt and Syria invaded Israel. First, the Arab oil states announced 17 percent price increases, bringing Saudi light crude to $3.65 a barrel. That having little effect, they turned to an embargo against the United States and the Netherlands. The impact was not immediate. Americans already had an oil crisis. They already had an "Energy Czar" and already had proposals for speed limits, car pools, gas taxes, and conservation incentives dressed as taxes. But with the embargo, all the moderate and "voluntary" measures turned severe. Solutions went from the national speed limit to "Gasless Sundays," to rationing, and "odd-even days" by which sales were limited to auto tags with odd or even first numbers. The lines and accompanying frustrations lasted through April, although the severity was regional and sporadic. When the shortages ended, the national speed limit did not. And neither did the "energy crisis," which carried on through the decade. The Ford and Carter administrations committed all the old mistakes and added many of their own. To promote "energy independence," domestic oil prices were set below imported crude. Only on his last day in office did President Ford sign an order to deregulate gasoline prices. Five days later, President Carter rescinded the order.

Come the overthrow of the Shah of Iran in January 1979, and it was October 1973 all over again. In April, Carter announced an end to the domestic crude limits that, at $6.00 a barrel, were ridiculously below the skyrocketing global prices that were broaching $30 on the spot markets. California was the first to return to the "odd-even" rationing that May, and the rest of the country soon followed. It was back to such things as drivers chasing around gasoline tankers and ramming gas lines. The crisis eased as the government's incremental price deregulation slowly brought order, but not before monumental confusion and day-long gas lines.

"NEVER … NEVER!"

- A Ford marketing executive when asked in 1975 if he'd ever seen such change in so little time.

If historical events tender themselves in hints well before their fuller expressions, we can see much of the larger decade of the 1970s at the New York automobile shows of 1969 and 1970. In '69 there was psychedelia and go-go. Robert Reisner showed off the "limousine of the future" that featured a TV, stereo, bar and automatic ice-maker in the back compartment he called "the pleasure capsule." It ran 23 feet, nearly half-again as long as the main commercial attraction of the show, the Maverick. The 1970 show would feature $250,000 "his and hers" Rolls-Royce limousines and a $13,500 Excalibur roadster. Hoping to catch some enthusiasm, AMC brought along its new subcompact, the Gremlin, and GM, not ready yet with its new little car, displayed the 4-cylinder engine that would go in it. Outside, protesters shouted out the end of the automobile.

The 1980 show was a world away. There were no go-go girls, and there were neither protests nor mod limousines. Subdued was as alive as it got. It was January 1980. Two domestic builders were in free fall. There wasn't even optimism among the importers, who knew exactly what was to follow their huge jump in sales. "It's like the joke about watching your mother-in-law go off a cliff in your new Cadillac," lamented an importers representative. Sure enough, the UAW demanded import quotas. But there was some good news. Luxury sales were up. At a time when it was news that luxury cars *still* sold, that Americans hadn't given up on self-indulgence and prestige marked hope. Others of more modest needs and taste would launch their own rebellions over getting what they wanted. Chrysler's salvation, the minivan, resurrected the family wagon. And that Dodge, GM and Ford sugar-daddy, the pickup truck, was already soaking up unhappy consumer demand made up of Mavericks, Vegas and Chevettes. And when Ford figured out how to defy CAFE standards and disguise a truck as a car, the SUV revolution was to be born. The American automobile would soon be back—the big American automobile, that is. **AQ**

One of the tragedies of the '70s: shrinking bodies. What was American styling's love child, the Ford Mustang was reduced to compact status. Stripped of muscle, the 1974 version.

APPERSON

Two Brothers Who Made the Rabbit Famous

Elmer *and Edgar Apperson comprised a turn-of-the-century automotive duo that stood in stark contrast with another famously talented fraternal pair of the period, the Duryea brothers. The internal strife between the Duryeas led to the end of that joint venture, whereas the Appersons worked in-step, maintaining a productive and important relationship until the elder brother died. The story of the brothers, their company and their cars is worthy of contemplation and appreciation.*

BY TRACY POWELL

The brothers were born and raised on the family's homestead three miles southeast of Kokomo. Elmer was the first, born on Aug. 13, 1861, to Elbert S. and Anna E. Apperson. Elmer attended district schools of Taylor Township, grade schools in Kokomo, and normal school in Valparaiso. Lifelong friend Edwin Souder recalled Elmer as a boy "roaming the woods and fields with dog and gun."

Elmer first arrived in Kokomo as a machinist apprentice, seeking to hone his natural ability to work with machinery, primarily farming implements. He later worked as a craftsman in railway shops near Kokomo, and then as a "machinist in charge, going year after year with threshermen into the great Northwest to help garner the harvest there." Elmer developed his managerial skills and "learned the mechanical trade" at Star Machine Works in Kokomo. In 1889, Elmer struck out on his own, starting Riverside Machine Works. Soon, Edgar, his younger brother by nine years, joined him at the shop where Elmer trained him in the trade.

The automotive destiny of the brothers began in autumn 1893, when a new arrival in Kokomo knocked on their shop door. It was Elwood Haynes, a 35-year-old with a background in science (see *Automobile Quarterly*, Vol. 38 No. 4, "Haynes-Apperson: Elwood Builds an Automobile"). In hand were drawings for a self-propelled vehicle, as well as a stationary single-cylinder, two-cycle Sintz marine engine Haynes had ordered that summer at the Chicago World's Fair. A friend had suggested approaching the Appersons, who ran Riverside Machine Works next to Wildcat Creek on South Main Street. The Appersons produced, among other things, bicycles and farm machinery, a well-equipped shop for Haynes' experiment.

Elmer took on the job, but with some skepticism at first. He worked on the car only after attending to regular customers, and for the going rate of 40 cents an hour. Elmer eventually handed the job over to Edgar, who couldn't get to the horseless carriage until November, after repairs had been completed on other customers' threshing machines. As months passed, Haynes would visit the shop with rec-

ommendations and adjustments to the engine. Haynes also suggested that the Appersons bring in more expertise, found in the person of Jonathan D. Maxwell, another local. As with Elmer, Maxwell had apprenticed at Star Machine Works. It appears that Maxwell had at one time worked at Riverside Machine Works. Finally, on the evening of July 3, 1894, the automobile was completed. The Appersons billed 59 1/2 hours of shop time.

Above: Riverside Machine Works. Right: Elwood Haynes in the Pioneer horseless carriage, 1894.

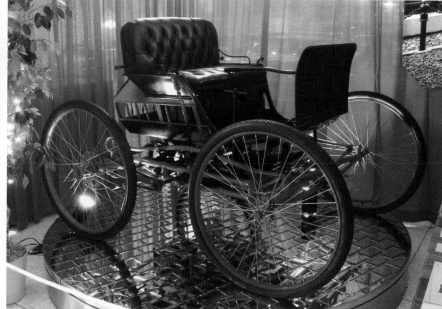

Above left: 1899 Haynes-Apperson. Above right: Pioneer II. Below: 1900 Haynes-Apperson.

According to Edgar Apperson in an interview in 1951, an open buggy body was purchased for $7 and bolted to the frame. Naturally, both the Appersons and Haynes wanted to test the vehicle as soon as they could the next day. That day was July 4, and Kokomo would be celebrating Independence Day, which meant a big crowd. The country was the best option, as curious onlookers crowded too closely for a safe start, so Haynes and his brother-in-law towed the horseless carriage out of town on a graveled lane called Pumpkinville Pike, the Apperson brothers following in their buggy. With Haynes at the wheel, the others push-started the motorized buggy, and one of America's first automobiles rumbled from the country and into Kokomo to the amazement—and some consternation—of the populace. That first horseless carriage reached 7 or 8 mph.

In 1895, Haynes and the Apperson brothers formed an informal partnership and set about building a new car especially for the Times-Herald race in Chicago, the first automobile race in America. The

new Haynes-Apperson auto was unable to start the Times-Herald race because it was damaged in an accident while proceeding to the starting line on race day morning. The Haynes-Apperson entry received a $150 prize for its meritorious design feature-the reduction of vibration by balancing the engine.

One of the few American petrol-engined cars in Britain at the time was a Haynes-Apperson "Four Passenger Pleasure Carriage" owned by Earl Russell, who drove it at various Automobile Club events. Russell allowed the editors of *The Autocar* to test drive his Haynes-Apperson. Their report in the Feb. 1, 1902, edition was filled with kudos: "The trip, though made in bad weather and over very heavy roads, impressed us with the comfort and reliability of the vehicle."

The editors noted that the ample-length elliptical springs made for a smooth ride on their 20-mile trip, during which "sufficient" gradients were climbed, "showing us how well and sweetly this car ran on

1901 Haynes-Apperson, with engine and registration plate.

its top speed without any necessity for changing." Despite the positive experience, the editors were pessimistic of its appeal to Continental buyers: "The vehicle is undoubtedly most efficient, controllable and comfortable, but on its present lines we fear it will hardly appeal to European taste, fashioned as that is upon prevailing French models."

The models did find a place among American buyers, however. The engine used on models from 1898 to 1901 was a two-cylinder, 7hp engine, set horizontally beneath the rear of the vehicle and featuring opposing cylinders, piston rods that worked on cranks on the engine shaft and set at 180 degrees in a cast-iron oil bath crank chamber. The reliability of this engine and its associated parts built a strong and steady reputation. Power was transmitted to the rear axle through cut steel and bronze gearing. A special friction clutch of their own design was used.

Production increased from three in 1897 to five the next year, when the Haynes-Apperson Automobile Company was organized. The Riverside Machine Works was transformed into a full-fledged automobile factory, eventually holding capacity for producing a car every two or three weeks. By the fall of 1898, the company moved operations to a new factory in Kokomo that effectively increased produc-

tion capacity to two cars a week. The two-cylinder engine was fitted to three models: carriages that carried two, four or six passengers. Prices ranged from $1,250 for the double-occupancy, to $1,500 for the four-passenger, to $1,600 for the six-passenger carriage.

The Haynes-Apperson catalog for these models noted that a six-passenger model was sold in Puerto Rico to carry the U.S. mail from San Juan to Ponce. The route was 80 miles and completed in 6-7 hours. It was also mentioned that a two-passenger "Doctor's Phaeton" (a phaeton purchased by New York physician Dr. Ashley Webber) had "made the longest continuous run yet made in America, the distance from Kokomo, Ind., to Brooklyn, N.Y. One thousand and fifty miles covered without an accident and the carriage was in perfect condition on its arrival at the end of the journey." Average speed for that trip was reportedly 14 mph.

Thirty models were produced in 1899. By 1900, production was full swing at the new facility, reaching 192 units. In 1901, the Kokomo-to-New York trip was repeated, this time in just 73 hours, which

Elwood Haynes said was a speed record. That same year, the Haynes-Apperson won a blue ribbon in the Long Island Endurance Run and two first prizes in the New York-Rochester Endurance Contest. By the end of the year, 240 Haynes-Appersons had been produced, but the Apperson brothers ended their partnership with Haynes, moving their operation back to the Riverside Machine Works building.

Leading up to the split, Elmer found himself flying solo in charge of the busy factory. Haynes was preoccupied with continued management of the Indiana Natural Gas and Oil Company, leaving Elmer overseeing 80-100 employees, with much more pressing responsibility than he was used to at a smaller machine shop. Dave Griffey writes in "Beyond the Pioneer" that it was perhaps for this reason that Elmer advised Edgar to quit his job and return to the Riverside building to begin drawings for a new automobile. Elmer promised he would join him later, which he did.

Some have said that the split was amicable. This theory holds that the Apperson brothers were following a similar trek of what Louis Chevrolet, Henry Ford and others would follow: speed is king, or, what became such a buzz phrase much later, "Race 'em on Sunday, sell 'em on Monday." Haynes, so the theory

Top: Haynes-Apperson factory, 1899. Left: Group of Apperson Company workers. There are 16 men and several carriages and carriage parts as well as an International Harvester planter.

Apperson Bros 1902 Models, Two Cyl

Above: Apperson test drivers, c. 1910, taken by the Apperson Brothers auto plant at Main St. and Park Ave. The driver on the far left is Harris M. Hanshue and on the far right is Herb Lytel. Right: The basketball team sponsored by the Apperson Automobile Co.

goes, was pushing for elegance.

Further evidence of a friendly parting of ways is seen in the prolonged use of Apperson's name on Haynes's cars. Although the Appersons left Haynes in 1901, models continued rolling out of the Haynes factory with the Haynes-Apperson label until mid-year 1904.

That the split was less than amicable is a more likely scenario. The quest to be known by history as the first automaker was idealized by both parties, evidently more so by Haynes who was first to wave his banner. Both Apperson and Haynes took pains to avoid mentioning the other in the press and in their advertising. Haynes was the first to use "America's First Motor Car" in his promotions, and in 1905 he submitted the 1894 model to the Smithsonian—without any mention of the Apperson brothers' contribution in the press release.

What's more, the reason for the prolonged use of the Haynes-Apperson name may be contributed to how Elmer Apperson was doled out his remaining

shares in the Haynes-Apperson company. It has been shown that before Elmer left, both Elwood Haynes and Elmer owned 59 percent of the company's stock. It's conceivable that Elmer was paid out over a matter of years while the cars still carried the combined name.

Tensions teetered on the edge of tribal warfare by 1913, when Elmer Apperson wrote to A.B. Armstrong, a civic influential in Kokomo, on June 19:

> There seems to be a little rivalry between the Haynes Automobile Company and ourselves in trying to get a license number from the Secretary of State for manufacturing under the new automobile law. The Haynes Company have applied for #1, and we also have asked the Secretary of State, Mr. L. G. Ellingham, to give us #1 license.
>
> We think that we have just as much right, or more, to this number as the Haynes Company. We are paying considerable more taxes in the State of Indiana than the Haynes Automobile Company, doing quite a little larger business, and in my opinion have just as much right to this number as they.
>
> If you should happen to know Mr. Ellingham, or any of your political friends, who could help in this matter, I can assure you that you would win a home with this company. I believe you will agree with me that we are just as much entitled to #1 license number as the above company, and another thing, it is a matter of pride to be able to get it "in preference to the other fellow."
>
> Knowing your ability in these lines, I am calling upon you for help, because I certainly want to put it over them on getting this number. We have already sent in our application and have written a letter to Mr. Ellingham on this subject, and if any action is taken, it must be done quickly.

In 1902, the Appersons were busy building cars, though at a much more scaled-down rate than that of Haynes-Apperson. The intention was to manufacture higher-priced, better quality, and fewer cars. By the end of their first year they had completed four cars with orders for several more. They continued using the two-cylinder Sintz engine, to which they were accustomed.

The following year, however, they changed to a four-cylinder to accommodate for the heavier cars. Elmer and Edgar stretched their chassis almost 30 inches beyond what their key competitor, Haynes-Apperson, offered. The first Apperson models cost $2,500, nearly twice that of Haynes-Apperson models, and production reached 163.

A larger four-cylinder engine was offered in 1904, powering a new seven-passenger touring sedan that cost $5,000, $2,000 more than the standard Apperson model. Total production hit 176 cars.

In 1905, production reached 194 and would have likely been more if not for a factory fire. The fire burned the building to the ground. Due to the construction of a new building, there were only 20 cars built for the 1906 model year. But the design for 1907 models was well underway, a design that would carve the course for Appersons for years to come. It was the Jack Rabbit.

Introduced in 1907, the Apperson Jack Rabbit was

In 1913, the State of Indiana issued its first "real" license plate, and Haynes and the Appersons both wanted the coveted No. 1. For this year only, license plates measured a mere 14.5 by 4.5 inches for ones utilizing five digits and was the only plate issued in Indiana that had a porcelain finish on a heavy metal base. From 1905 through 1912, a circular disk about the size of a half-dollar on the front of the car was a permanent registration that cost a dollar from the Secretary of State. (Motorists were required to make registration medallions themselves, or have them produced by a local blacksmith.) Of the approximately 41,000 plates issued in 1913, it is unclear who received the first one.

Top left: Edgar Apperson in the Apperson "Jack Rabbit" in Chicago at the Vanderbilt Cup Races in 1904. Above: 1909 Apperson. Left: Two cars on the Apperson Brothers' loading dock.

guaranteed to run 75 mph, an attractive proposition for those with a thirst for speed. The racy runabout with a round gas tank on the rear deck was a popular model. Production ramped back up, this time to 183 cars for the year. Although a Jack Rabbit never won a major race, souped-up versions placed high

"This was the year the Haynes management realized Apperson was a real competitor, and a new public controversy would soon begin between the companies."

company and the Appersons were doing well: each brother was making $5,000 on salary, and the factory produced 247 cars before the end of 1908. That number increased to 312 the next year, when cash on hand was recorded as $100,228 with $10,000 more in accounts receivables. Accounts payable was only

Edgar (left), Elmer (right) and the Apperson Brothers Automobile Company plant (above).

in big-name venues such as the Vanderbilt Cup and Fairmount Park. A Jack Rabbit racer was offered as a limited-production car in 1907.

Apperson Brothers Automobile Co. was incorporated on Nov. 14, 1908, with $400,000 in capital stock. Listed as directors of the corporation were Edgar (as president and general manager), Elmer (as vice president) and Alton G. Seiberling (as secretary-treasurer). C.H. Felske was listed as director.

Seiberling was an important backer to the young enterprise. He hailed from a prominent Kokomo family, which came from Akron, Ohio, after natural gas was discovered in Kokomo in 1886. The gas was a natural resource free for the taking for interested companies. The patriarch, Monroe Seiberling, founded the Kokomo Strawboard Co., and, eventu-

ally, the Diamond Plate Glass Co. (later to become PPG). The Seiberling Mansion is now home to the Howard County Historical Museum.

For reasons not entirely clear, and in an interesting nod to the intense competition between the Appersons and Haynes, Alton Seiberling had previously been the superintendent at the Haynes company since 1905. Now, in 1908, he was the production manager for the Appersons. Seiberling later left the Appersons to re-join Haynes in his venture in September 1912. (In 1923, he was listed as vice president and general manager of The Haynes Automobile Company.)

Six-cylinder engines were introduced in 1908 for two models, but the six wasn't mass-produced (relatively speaking) in Appersons until 1914. The

$29,657, which paints a rosy financial picture.

By 1910, the Apperson plant was cranking out almost as many cars as was cross-town rival Haynes, helped no doubt from the drop in the Jack Rabbit's price, down to $4,250. According to author Dave Griffey, "This was the year the Haynes management realized Apperson was a real competitor, and a new public controversy would soon begin between the companies."

RACING APPERSONS

The need for speed was captured by the Jack Rabbit. Appearances in an event called the Cobe Cup race were notable. The 395-mile

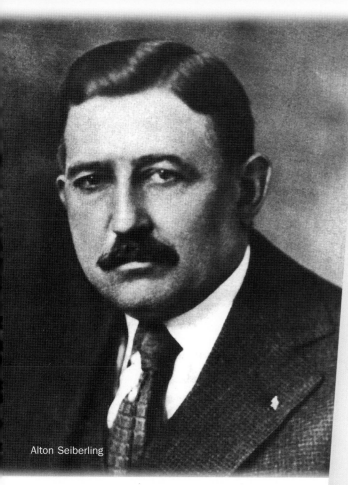
Alton Seiberling

four-cylinder Jack Rabbit in the 1911 Indy 500. The race, also called the International 500-Mile Sweepstakes Race at the time, was the first recorded automobile race of such distance in history. The largest racing purse offered to that date, $27,550, drew 46 entries from the United States and Europe, from which 40 qualified by sustaining 75 mph for a

WARNING

NOTICE TO MANUFACTURERS OF EXPLOSION ENGINES USED FOR ANY PURPOSE:

I am the owner of the Letters Patent of United States No. 617,806, granted to F. E. Canda January 17, 1899, for electric Igniter for Explosion Engines, and Letters Patent No. 905,625 granted to Elmer Apperson December 1, 1908, for improvements in Explosion Engines.

Briefly stated, these patents cover broadly the use of two or more separate electric igniting devices, provided with separate circuits and means for throwing the igniting devices into or out of action simultaneously or independently; as well as covering the use of two or more spark plugs or sparking points having electrical connection with a magneto and battery with means of throwing the spark plugs or points into or out of operation.

Motor illustrating Apperson system of Ignition under Patents 617,806 and 905,625

All persons now using or desiring to use this system of ignition are invited to negotiate with me. I have no desire to unnecessarily embarrass any one, but *infringers* on my patents will be legally and vigorously prosecuted.

ELMER APPERSON,
c\o APPERSON BROS. AUTOMOBILE COMPANY,
KOKOMO, IND.

This interesting message ran in the January 1909 issue of *Motor* as a full-page ad. At the time, manufacturers were paying a royalty to the Association of Licensed Automobile Manufacturers for use of the Selden patent (see *Automobile Quarterly*, Vol. 4 No. 3, "I Invented the Automobile: The Eight-Year War Over the Selden Patent"). It appears that the Appersons sought their own royalty arrangement. Regardless, as a partial result of the lengthy Selden lawsuits, the groundwork for industry standardization took hold within two years of this ad placement, limiting such claims to patent sovereignty.

Cobe Cup race was held on July 19, 1909. The course was 23.27 miles per lap, winding through the northern Indiana towns of Crown Point, Lowell and Cedar Lake. The race was staged by The Chicago Automobile Club in an effort to create a western Vanderbilt Cup-type race. There was an international flavor, as a Fiat was entered to race domestic-factory entries of Apperson, Buick, Locomobile, Knox and Stoddard-Dayton. Louis Chevrolet, driving on the Buick racing team, took the lead on the fourth lap and won the race with 65 seconds to spare. The following year the Cobe Cup race moved to Indianapolis. The year after came the debut of a 500-mile marathon that would also be held in Indianapolis, where the Jack Rabbit showed up again.

Herb Lytle, test driver for Apperson, drove a

quarter-mile distance, though starting position was determined by date of entry instead of speed. Lytle started in 31st position. When he crashed during pitting on his 83rd lap, he was out, finishing 32 out of the field of 40.

In 1911, all four models were now referred to as Apperson Jack Rabbit models, ranging from $2,000 to $4,200. The factory was now nearing the 1,000-car production milestone.

The Apperson brothers again entered a racing model in the Indianapolis 500 in 1912. But while they were with Lytle and the mechanic attending to a flat tire a safe distance from the track, another car slid out of control at an estimated 90 mph and crashed into the car. None of the four were injured, but the car was out of commission. Elmer was convinced that the race wasn't safe enough to try again, and he never returned with an entry.

The public controversy alluded to earlier began this year. Haynes fired the first shot, advertising his wares as "America's First Car." Soon thereafter the Appersons began using the slogan "Building Cars Since 1893." Fierce competition was fueled by other manufacturers during this period as well, forcing the Appersons to reposition its Jack Rabbit brand. The roadster was now priced at $1,600, almost $3,000 less than its previous sticker. Elmer's business acumen paid off: assets jumped to more than $2.3 million in 1913, and the company expanded its plant the next year.

In 1914, the Jack Rabbit entry in the Grand Prix represented the last appearance of a chain-driven car in a major U.S. racing event. But Elmer was already looking ahead to a new powerplant.

THE APPERSON ASCENT

A new engine was designed in 1915, a V8 with 80 less parts than a conventional engine. It was the new Apperson Eight. A vee-shaped radiator also appeared late in the year. According to Griffey, requests for Apperson cars were higher than

Above: Herb Lytle with his mechanic at Indy in 1911. Below: The Apperson in 1914.

the company could produce. This came as a result of wide public acceptance and dealer kudos of the styling and engineering of the Eight.

Material and men moved to a newly constructed plant north of the Riverside location, which had been prone to flooding from the adjacent creek. Still in Kokomo, the new plant featured new equipment, and the move was planned to be a smooth transition. Work did indeed continue unabated, as 1916 proved to be the most proliferate year for the Appersons: a total of 1,817 cars were manufactured. All four-cylinder models were dropped from the line. At the time, assets were tallied at more than $4.6 million, and a 25-percent dividend was paid on the spot. Prosperous times indeed.

When America entered World War I, supplies shrank, and the Appersons suffered along with other car makers. But the large amount of cash on hand allowed the company to buffet the storm. In 1917, Elmer had a stroke, forcing him to slow down and take his hands off the reigns. For how long was unknown. Edgar stepped in immediately to assume

his brother's position at the plant, and he soon adopted Elmer's title as general manger, although Elmer retain his president's title.

> Beauty is more than skin deep. It proceeds from the 58 Horsepower, eight cylinder motor, the balance that affords easy riding and driving, the harmonious relation of parts that insures years of certain and effective service. Investigate. Sixes and Eights. Touring Cars and "Chummy" Roadsters.
>
> From an Apperson ad in *Motor Life*, October 1917

Elmer's stroke kept him out of the plant for about two years. During this time, with Edgar in charge and making $18,000 in salary, sentiment was growing about the stale appeal of the Jack Rabbit moniker. A new model was introduced in 1918 as the Roadaplane to replace the Jack Rabbit. But that name was dropped after lackluster sales, and Jack Rabbits were back on the badging before the year was out.

C.T. Silver, a New York Apperson dealer, designed some of the most eye-stopping Appersons. These specials featured uninterrupted lines along the body-

Above left: Apperson ad from 1918 touting the Apperson 8 with its engine of "80 less parts." Right: The 1919 Tourister, top down. Below: A 1919 model with body by Shutte.

work, as well as bullet headlamps and oval radiators. These specials carried the "Silver" name for 1918, and the styling continued into the next decade.

Production fell off while Elmer was away, and executives circulated the whys and wherefores of "excessive facilities" and fewer cars rolling out of the factory. But Apperson was far from down and out. In 1919, Elmer returned to an increased salary of $30,000. Edgar's position also now paid $30,000. It was well known that Bob Hope purchased his first automobile this year, a Jack Rabbit.

BEGINNING OF THE END

On March 27, 1920, Elmer died of a heart attack at age 58. He was attending an automobile race in Los Angeles. An obituary in the *Indianapolis Star*, dated March 30, summed up the great loss to the industry: "He was one of the comparatively few in the industry who, by their confidence, energy and courage, have brought the

"He always wanted the car that bore his name to have individuality and distinction. He had originality and not a little of the artist nature, and he always put into his product something of himself."

Rear view of the Ace model of 1924.

automobile from nothing to perfection, from a toy to a necessity, within a generation."

The news was devastating to Edgar and the company. In a tribute to Elmer, Edwin Souder ("Boyhood's playmate, manhood's friend") wrote: "He always wanted the car that bore his name to have individuality and distinction. He had originality and not a little of the artist nature, and he always put into his product something of himself."

Now the product had to go on without Elmer's influence in engineering, styling and business management. Elmer's wife, Catherine, was named to replace Elmer on the board of directors. Edgar became the president and general manager, and he oversaw the opening of a new office building in Kokomo. The offices were finished in black walnut with black marble wainscoting, and featured a

marble entrance hall floor with a jackrabbit imbedded into the center.

Production increased to over 1,000 cars, the best year since 1917. To counter overhead expenses, the company increased prices in 1921, only to lower them again in 1922 to try to jump-start sales. A new speedster was introduced for $2,620, with three additional models for under $3,500.

But the writing was on the wall. Production for 1922 slumped to 613. For the first time in the company's history, outside capital was sought. According

to the abstract associated with the acquisition of outside capital, the company's stock was valued at $4.1 million in 1922. Company officials thought the partial stock sale would stave off the cash crunch, but interest waned in the stock. Buyers were few.

The strategy to increase cash flow consisted of converting the excess number of unsold finished cars – valued at a cost of more than $318,000 – to discounted models. Prices for these models, along with 1923 models, were slashed by 30 percent. The strategy calculated that 1,800 cars sold – a high projection indeed, topping record sales -- at the discounted prices would yield a profit, but only 748 cars actually sold. This low sales volume was not a reflection of the quality of car, but a reality facing the entire industry.

Above: This Apperson automobile was referred to as "Glove Finish Sport Coupe." The photo was taken from a postcard; on the back is written: "Apperson—All Weather—Glove Finish Coupe—With the famous Mechanical Gear Shift—This new type body is the greatest development in design, finish and construction in the history of automobile building—Enduring weather proof fabric over a frame of resilient, expanded steel. Light—Easy riding and always NEW. —Straight-Away 8 Super Valve 6." Right: An ad that ran in *Motor*, 1923.

The Apperson Car, the Factory and the Policy

There is, to-day, no sentiment in the automobile business. If a dealer can't make money out of a car, he drops it. He is in business to make money—not to satisfy the sales ambitions of the factory or merely because it gives him prestige to represent a well known car—his job is to *make money*. Therefore, the intelligent, far-sighted dealer is, to-day, *thinking for himself*.

As a matter of self preservation he is sizing up his present line *and other cars* purely on the basis of how much money he can make in 1923—and thereafter.

He is vitally interested in the car, the factory and the factory policy. He knows that he has got to have a car that will sell—and stay sold. A car that will make a better demonstration than other cars; and then run longer, more smoothly and satisfactorily with less trouble and at less expense than other cars. A car that looks better and *is better*. A car that is so correctly engineered and conscientiously built that it does not eat up all the profit on service. Finally, he must have a car with a clean history—a car whose engineering record has no black spots on it. SUCH A CAR IS THE APPERSON.

Behind the car he must have a strong, clean, square-dealing factory, whose word is as good as its bond. A factory whose past calls for no explanations or apologies. A factory big enough to

make all the cars he can sell and deliver them in A-1 condition ON TIME. SUCH A FACTORY IS BEHIND THE APPERSON.

The successful dealer must have a factory policy that is based on the one idea of the prosperity of the dealer. A factory policy that does not shove cars down his throat, does not ride him, does not make him stretch his financial facilities to the cracking point. Does not break him. A factory policy that backs him up and makes him strong with his banker. SUCH A POLICY IS THAT OF THE APPERSON.

These things being true of Apperson, this car, this factory and the Apperson policy commend themselves to those intelligent dealers who are out in 1923 to make money.

See the new Apperson Six and Eight at the New York Show, January 6th to 13th, in Space B-15, and at the Chicago Show, January 27th to February 3rd, in Space A-4 at the Armory.

APPERSON BROS. AUTOMOBILE CO.
Kokomo, Indiana, U.S.A.

In a letter dated April 26, 1923, from Clarence Werner in the sales department, Werner touts the worthiness of Apperson's eight-cylinder models to a potential customer:

"We believe we have made a successful anticipation of the wishes of the average motorist and are furnishing accessory equipment harmonizing with the car and adding greatly to its appearance. We have never offered the public a bad model ... or a car that was not as nearly perfect as anything mechanical can be thought to be."

The Apperson Eight had become the firm's mainstay. But the company was eager to acquire an off-the-shelf six to become a player in that field. In late 1923 a new six-cylinder was introduced with a Falls engine.

By this time, lenders were becoming wary of the company's ability to turn the ship around. Assets

were wrapped up in buildings, new cars and equipment, but the crippled cash flow was alarming. Gradually, as loans failed to be secured, the outside investors capitalized on a stock-surrender agreement in which ownership changed hands.

Throughout 1924, as the company's financial situation bottomed, the board petitioned to change the firm's name to the Pioneer Automobile Company. Excess and obsolete equipment was auctioned off. Yet the company dealerships managed to sell 682 cars during the year.

In January 1925, Edgar sat next to a handful of automotive pioneers who were honored at the New York Silver Jubilee Automobile Show's Manufacturers' Dinner. The image holds several ironies. Edgar was the only one pictured still actively involved in the operations of his respective company, but almost

exactly a year later Apperson Brothers Automobile Co. would be no more. Joining him in the seats of honor were notables such as John Maxwell, with whom he had worked, greasy hands and all, in the pioneer days. Elwood Haynes is also in the picture; he would die just four months later from pneumonia, an event that sealed the fate of The Haynes Automobile Co.

The new management at Apperson closed the small but healthy dealership network, and opened three dealer outlets called "factory outlets" in Los

Above and left: Front and interior of the 1923 Apperson.
Right: The 1920 Apperson 8.

Angeles, Chicago and New York City. These outlets were open seven days a week, 24 hours a day. The goal was to produce as many cars as possible and sell them as quickly as possible. Apperson's long-time name recognition would have been a prize for the East Coast money interest.

Later in the year, as the straight-eight craze swept the country, a Lycoming engine supplemented Apperson's V8 line. The Jack Rabbit was again applied, this time to the Lycoming-powered Eight. Another addition to 1926 models was the introduction of front wheel brakes. These models would be the company's last.

THE DISENCHANTED BROTHER

Apperson Brothers Automobile Co. went into receivership on Jan. 12, 1926. The plant sale on July 20-22 resulted in new tenants in the factory and offices. J.M. Leach Manufacturing Co. moved in after Oct. 25, 1926. In 1937, Northern Indiana Supply Co., a wholesale distributor of industrial supplies, moved into the buildings, where it remains today.

After the company failed, Edgar and his wife Inez moved to Wisconsin. And they wintered in Phoenix. Back in 1916, Edgar had visited a good friend who had relocated to Phoenix for health reasons, and Edgar liked the area so well that he purchased some land. He had also invested in a company, which he helped found around 1920, called the Arizona Storage and Distributing Company.

Above: 1923 Apperson Touring. Right: Edgar Apperson in later years. Inset: One of the last advertisements for Apperson cars, this appeared in *Motor* in 1924.

Now he lived in the climate he loved. Edgar was an avid outdoorsman, and especially enjoyed fishing. In the late '30s, Edgar and Inez were involved in a nearly fatal automobile accident. As Inez explained in a letter to her sister, a drunk driver broadsided Inez's "pet Packard that Ed built for me." Edgar was not seriously hurt, but Inez suffered a triple skull fracture.

It was evident that Edgar had lost interest in the automobile business as early as 1920, perhaps before his brother had died. On April 3, 1923, Edgar stated to the board that he wished to be relieved of all executive responsibilities and resigned as president. He did, however, continue working in engineering and development. He and Inez had already sold their home and listed their residence as a hotel in Kokomo. Plans were evidently in place to move to the Southwest.

Also in April 1923, floating bonds and cheap stock

1893

Into the thirty-first year

Ever since the building of the first practical automobile by Apperson Brothers in 1893, the name Apperson has stood for fine engineering—fine workmanship.

Thirty years of engineering—thirty years of hammering cars over the road, have produced a car which is representative of the best engineering developments in the industry.

Apperson goes into its thirty-first year with the finest cars in its history. The Apperson Eight and the Apperson Six, both with mechanical *gear-shift*, are the aristocratic descendants of the first practical automobile built in America—the greatest achievement of an engineer who has placed engineering above everything in his endeavor to build *worthily* rather than in great numbers.

The MECHANICAL GEAR-SHIFT, standard equipment on all Apperson models, does away with shifting and emergency brake levers.

See these cars at the Shows.

We have a co-operative franchise and your territory may be open.

APPERSON BROS. AUTOMOBILE COMPANY
KOKOMO, INDIANA

NEW YORK SHOW
SPACE 2

CHICAGO SHOW
SPACE A-27 A-28

APPERSON
Built on KNOWLEDGE

APPERSON

deals effectively pushed all the original owners and management out of the loop of control. At that time, George H. Burr & Company, the new stockholders, controlled Apperson Brothers Automobile Co. Although he remained on the board of directors, Edgar was completely powerless in regards to corporate decision making. It likely wouldn't have mattered if he could call some of the shots. Creditors, including engine suppliers and body makers, were clamoring for past-due payments, and supplies stopped pending cash receipts.

Edgar Apperson died in Phoenix in 1959.

It is clear that after Elmer's death, the company faltered. As Griffey puts it, "The death of the company was certain because of its small size, but poor management sped up the demise. Edgar had never made the business a top priority. It seemed to fall somewhere below hunting, fishing and other personal business ventures." AQ

HARLEY EARL

BILL MITCHELL

IRV RYBICKI

ED WELBURN

CHUCK JORDAN

WAYNE CHERRY

The Dynasty of Design

O nly six people have headed General Motors Design in 80 years, between 1927 and 2006. Their succession is unbroken. The power and the prerogatives they have created for themselves have at times been regal. Their line traces back to the beginning of automotive styling itself.

BY LEIGH DORRINGTON

HARLEY EARL 1927–1958

arley J. Earl was first; the larger-than-life figure who created the General Motors design dynasty. It hardly seems possible to contain the accomplishments of this human dynamo in his 31 years at General Motors in words.

The creation of automobile styling as a profession, the "dream car", General Motors' Motorama and the Chevrolet Corvette are only a few of Harley Earl's credits. Under Earl's leadership GM ruled the industry. He said he designed for the future and let others catch up. The introduction of tail fins, the hardtop roof and wraparound windshield were widely imitated. He helped to achieve Alfred P. Sloan's ideal of "dynamic obsolescence". And, in doing so, he helped to make General Motors the largest automaker in the world.

Harley Earl was born in Los Angeles, California in 1893 where his father, J.W. Earl, was the proprietor of a successful coach and carriage company (*Automobile Quarterly* Vol. 20, No. 1). He joined the family firm—which became the Earl Automobile Works in 1908—as a designer and superintendent. He was soon specializing in designing custom automobiles for the new movie community in Hollywood.

The Earl Automobile Works also created custom body designs for the Don Lee Company, the Los Angeles Cadillac distributor. In 1920, Don Lee acquired the Earl company with 27-year old Harley Earl as manager. The large number of orders coming from Don Lee for un-bodied chassis attracted the attention of the Cadillac Motor Car Company, whose General Manager was Lawrence Fisher—one of the brothers of Fisher Body. Fisher traveled to California to learn how Cadillac chassis going to Don Lee were being used. He was impressed with what he saw.

At the time, General Motors was planning a companion car to Cadillac, named the LaSalle (*Automobile Quarterly* Vol. 5, No. 3). Fisher offered

Harley Earl before joining General Motors: Before boarding an ocean liner (right) and his body work seen on a 1933 Cadillac coupe.

Above: Earl's hand was first best known for its touch on the LaSalle. Below: The first concept (or "show") car, also the work of Earl, the 1938 Buick Y-Job.

Earl a contract to come to Detroit to design the La Salle. The result, introduced in 1927, was one of the most successful new cars in automotive history up until that time.

The 1927 LaSalle has been described as the first car designed by a stylist, not engineers. It was exactly what General Motors president Alfred P. Sloan had in mind. Within the year, Sloan had hired Earl full time to create the General Motors Art and Colour Section, the first automotive styling staff in the industry. Sloan gave Earl only one instruction, "Make cars that sell."

Earl created the first professional styling studio at GM with 50 employees in 1928. He organized studios for each of General Motors' brands—Cadillac, Buick, Oldsmobile, Pontiac and Chevrolet. Each studio was charged with creating a separate brand identity, and was kept secret from competing studios. Only Earl and the studio head had a key to the door.

Earl managed by providing critical input to his staff and often carried ideas from one studio to another. He ruled by the force of his personality and towered over most of his contemporaries at 6 feet 4 1/2 inches. He dressed in colorful, expensive suits, shirts and ties that stood out like a beacon at GM. Harley Earl could also be a terrifying personality to those who worked for him—even his favorites. "Wonderful personality. Powerful," Bill Mitchell who succeeded Earl as vice president of design at GM said in 1984. "God, I admired (him). He just knocked the tar out of anybody. He'd get it fixed."

In 1937 The Art and Colour Section was re-named General Motors Design. Earl was made a Vice President of General Motors. GM continued to attract the best designers in the business, particularly as the Great Depression worsened through the 1930s. Earl and his staff created the first "dream car" in 1938. The "Y-Job" integrated fenders and body with complex compound curves and eliminated running boards. Electric windows and a power-operated top were a few of the advanced features displayed on the car. Earl drove the Y-Job on the streets of Detroit as his personal transportation.

Above left: The 1949 Cadillac Series 62. Above right: Earl shares a laugh with Mitchell and other GM execs. Below: An American icon a la Earl, by way of Zora Arkus-Duntov: The 1953 Chevrolet Corvette.

The Cadillac Series Sixty Special was another landmark design of the pre-World War II years. Earl and William Mitchell's Cadillac Studio designed the Series Sixty Special for 1938 and, like the Y-Job, forecast many features that would become widespread. The car was lower than previous models, and the absence of running boards enabled the designers to extend the body to the full width of the wheels. The trunk was made an integral part of the body. Doors with narrow pillars surrounding the glass predicted the "hardtop" roof Cadillac would introduce in the post-war years.

New designs were slow in coming following World War II. The 1948-49 Cadillacs led with innovative design elements like the hardtop roof and tail fins. Both were quickly copied throughout the industry. Selected members of Earl's design staff had been given a secret look at the Lockheed P-38 fighter plane early in the war, and the influence of the plane's twin tails could easily be seen in the post-war Cadillac designed by Franklin Q. Hershey.

The inspiration for the 1951 "LeSabre" concept car was pure jet aircraft. Like the Y-Job, the LeSabre forecast GM styling and new technologies

for the next decade, displaying use of lightweight metals, electronics and alternate fuels. And given Earl's status within General Motors, he once again adopted the LeSabre—a car built at an estimated cost of $7 million to GM shareholders—as his personal transportation.

Earl's styling studios produced a series of stunning new concept cars annually that today bring record prices at collector car auctions. In addition to early "Motorama" cars, Earl's Firebird I, II and III stand as highlights of 1950s thinking showcasing turbine technology in a series of aircraft shapes.

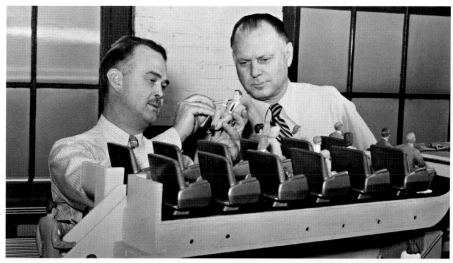
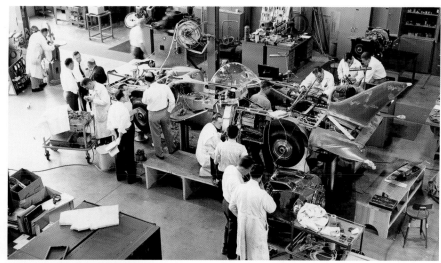

Above left: Earl with Irv Rybicki. Above right: Construction of the Firebird. Below: The GM Motorama was another Earl creation.

Dream cars became a highlight of the GM Motorama, another of Earl's innovations. The Motorama was GM's private auto show, staged eight times between 1949 and 1961. Nearly 10 million people attended shows that mixed the unrestrained enthusiasm of concept cars with the excitement of new GM production cars and musical productions that rivaled Broadway shows.

The Chevrolet Corvette was introduced at the 1953 Motorama. The Corvette began as another Harley Earl project, although Zora Arkus-Duntov is often credited with the car. Author Jerry Burton in his book *Zora Arkus-Duntov, The Legend Behind Corvette* explains that Earl conceived and created the Corvette at GM largely in secret in 1951 and 1952. Zora Arkus-Duntov saw the Corvette for the first time displayed at the 1953 GM Motorama at the Waldorf-Astoria hotel in New York.

By March 1956 over 700 artists and craftsmen worked in GM Design. In an interview with the *New York Times,* Earl described his role in the studio. "All I do is move around and stir things up a bit," he said. His designers, it seemed, saw his role differently. "A by-word among GM stylists (was) that once a design has been given final approval, 'Get the car out of styling before Mr. Earl starts approving it again.'"

Earl oversaw the creation of the massive General Motors Technical Center in Warren, Mich., conceiving the idea, selecting the site and commissioning architect Eero Saarinen. A feature story in

Earl with his Firebirds, the epitome of flight-inspired design. Below: The 1959 Cadillac Eldorado.

Exner, briefly upstaged General Motors long-established design leadership.

Harley Earl's designs accurately reflect the American character in the 1950s. They were "cars that sold" and GM ruled the industry.

After Harley Earl's retirement from General Motors, the active heads of design for General Motors (William Mitchell), Chrysler (Virgil Exner), Ford (Eugene Bordinat) and American Motors (Richard Teague) had all worked with Earl at GM.

In the years following his retirement, later GM executives sometimes seemed intent on discrediting Harley Earl's designs and the influence he exerted at General Motors. A review of the first book published about Harley Earl's years at General Motors appeared in the *Wall Street Journal* in 1984. Although the review is generally critical, one com-

LIFE magazine described the new Tech Center as a "Versailles of Industry" when it opened in May 1956. Many of the interiors and furnishings were considered ultramodern for their time.

Outside of General Motors, Harley Earl also established himself as one of the leaders in the new field of industrial design opening his own firm in 1945. Earl's grandson, Richard, confirms that Harley Earl had an offer to join Ford following World War II and the design firm may have been another indulgence from Alfred P. Sloan to keep him at GM.

Auto racing was also a significant influence on Harley Earl's imagination. Photos show him at a variety of race events and his son Jerry drove a Corvette SR2 race car prepared in one of Earl's GM studios. Following his retirement from GM, Harley Earl became the Commissioner of NASCAR in 1960. The Harley J. Earl Trophy is still presented to the winner of the Daytona 500.

Motorama concept cars influenced styling excesses that characterize many of the automobiles produced in the 1950s. But some of the cars designed in the Earl studios and produced in the 1950s are among

the best designs of the time. The early Cadillac Eldorado, the first Corvettes, the 1953 Buick Skylark and the 1955-57 Chevrolets are viewed as modern classics today. Others missed the mark. The entire 1959 GM car line was restyled while Earl was in Europe when the "Forward Look" 1957 Chrysler products, designed by former GM employee Virgil

ment is particularly revealing: "GM is ashamed of the Earl-era cars."

Symbols of Earl's influence at GM were unceremoniously discarded. Art and architectural features commissioned by Earl for the lobby of the Styling Administration building were sawed up and carried off.

BILL MITCHELL 1959-1977

William L. Mitchell described Harley Earl as "like a father to me. I was 23 when I started with him, and I was 46 when he turned it over to me. That was half of my life."

Mitchell's life and tenure at General Motors rivaled Harley Earl's. In 1959 he inherited Earl's office, his private dining room and the largest design staff in the industry—over 1,100 employees. He had known for five years that he would have the job and he increasingly influenced the future of GM designs in Earl's later years.

Mitchell joined the GM Art and Colour Section in 1935 and was in charge of the Cadillac studio by the following year. Strother MacMinn described Mitchell's career in *Automobile Quarterly*, Vol. 26, No. 2. "It took less than a year for Earl to recognize that the infectious humor and brash adventurism in

Above: Bill Mitchell was groomed for succession of the GM Design Chief spot. His love for speed complemented his knack for successful styling. He could be found testing Corvette concepts (with the above) as well as designing them, such as the 1961 Mako Shark (left). He also led the roll-out effort of the 1963 Buick Riviera (right).

Mitchell's personality reflected the design spirit that Earl needed."

Mitchell shared credit for the 1938 Cadillac Sixty Special. The 1948-49 Cadillac was locked-in when Mitchell returned from the Navy following World War II, but he was influential in many of the car's design elements. From 1949 to 1953, Mitchell left

GM to manage Harley Earl's industrial design firm, where he said he learned to 'sell' design.

When he returned to GM, Mitchell had significant influence on the Motorama cars. "We'd have twenty special cars—work our brains (out) and enjoyed it. There was an esprit de corps in the whole place," he said in a 1984 interview with David Crippen for

the Automotive Design Oral History project of the Henry Ford Museum. "Now it's a bore over there."

Mitchell did not like committees. "You don't get anywhere with a committee," he said. "Henry Ford made what he wanted." And Bill Mitchell seemed to agree.

The Corvette Sting Ray was an example of

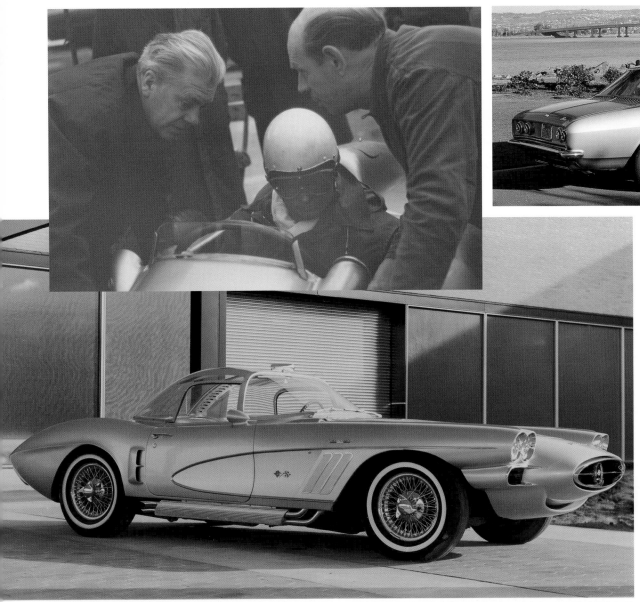

Left: Mitchell with Rudi Uhlenhaut during a Mercedes test drive. Above: The 1965 Corvair. Below: The experimental Corvette XP70.

The Sting Rays were always Bill Mitchell's cars. He told Chuck Jordan, his design director, "Don't ever forget, kid, you don't do the Corvettes. I do the Corvettes."

Other designs that characterized Mitchell's influence as the head of GM Design include the 1963 Buick Riviera—his favorite—the 1965 Chevrolet Corvair, 1966 Oldsmobile Toronado and the 1967 Cadillac Eldorado. The entire line of GM's 1965 cars stands out as Mitchell's best. The 1970 Camaro and Firebird, with their lean European look, were favorably compared to Ferraris. And the 1977 Caprice and Impala reflected dramatically changing design priorities following the 1973-74 oil embargo. Mitchell thought of styling as tailoring a car and described his designs as the "sheer" look, with wide smooth surfaces divided by sharp creases.

Bill Mitchell's concept cars were focused mainly on the future of the Corvette. General Motors and Zora Arkus-Duntov actively explored new layouts and technologies for the Corvette throughout the 1960's and '70s including rear-engine, mid-engine and transverse-engine designs, as well as rotary power. Each of these ideas found their way into a series of stunning concepts that an excited public hoped to see go into production year after year. Finally the 1977 Aerovette was approved at the very

Mitchell's independent streak. He built the first Sting Ray in 1959 with the help of stylist Larry Shinoda—and a design originated by Peter Brock in 1957—on a Corvette SS race car chassis he bought from GM for $500. Mitchell entered the Sting Ray in Sports Car Club of America races with Dick Thompson as the driver. They won the 1960 SCCA C Modified National Championship and Bill Mitchell drove the Sting Ray to work.

GM noticed. The Sting Ray directly influenced the Mako Shark show car that previewed the production Corvette Sting Ray introduced as a 1963 model.

end of Bill Mitchell's tenure at GM Design, only to be cancelled by new management.

Bill Mitchell was passionate about automobiles, racing and motorcycles all his life. He was an artist. He believed "cars should be beautiful," and the influence of earlier classics can be seen in many of his designs. In his 1984 interview Mitchell said, "Earl was the golden days, and I got the last of the golden days." After his retirement from GM in 1977 he refused invitations to visit GM styling studios, comment on new designs or speak to groups of young designers. He distained the engineering influence and committee systems, and the cars they produced. "I know Earl would roll over in his grave."

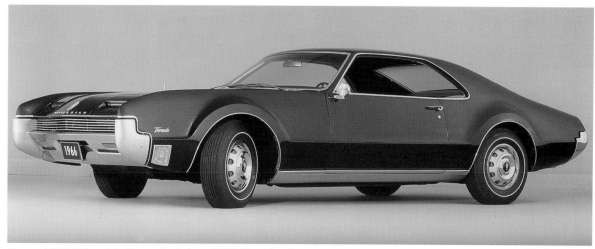

Above: 1966 Oldsmobile Toronado. Below: 1970 Chevrolet Camaro.

IRV RYBICKI 1977–1986

Speculation surrounding who would become the next Vice President of Design centered on Chuck Jordan and Irv Rybicki. Many suggest that—by winning the job—Rybicki was the one who lost.

Harley Earl and Bill Mitchell presented mythic figures at General Motors. If Harley Earl couldn't convince or bully the head of one of GM's divisions, he would simply reach for the telephone and say, "Well, let's see what Mr. Sloan thinks." Earl protected Bill Mitchell in a similar way. Mitchell could be as volatile as Harley Earl, but his greatest strength—in addition to his design talent—was his humor.

Dave Holls, a GM designer who co-authored *A Century of Automotive Style* with Michael Lamm wrote, "People who worked for and with Bill Mitchell either liked him or hated him. There weren't many on the fence. And yet he had this wonderful sense of humor and a light touch that Earl couldn't match."

Chuck Jordan was Mitchell's choice for the job. Jordan "could be charming and witty but, like Mitchell, he tended to be unpredictable. Unlike Mitchell, he didn't have a humorous side to soothe or smooth over the hurts." Irv Rybicki was more reserved and courtly. Stan Wilan, another Mitchell

designer, said, "If you asked anyone in the building who was going to replace Bill Mitchell, I think everybody—everybody—would have said Chuck. He was clearly the better designer, had better taste and more energy, commanded more respect and worked harder."

The difference was that Mitchell's independence and reputation as a loose cannon had caught up with him—and with Chuck Jordan. Others saw an opportunity to reign in the gratuitous excess of the Earl and Mitchell eras.

Irv Rybicki was named vice president of design

55

Above: The Aerovette. Above right: Mitchell's thirst for excitement never waned. Here, he sits atop one of his custom motorcycles. Below: Mitchell in the studio with Rybicki and the Stingray in clay.

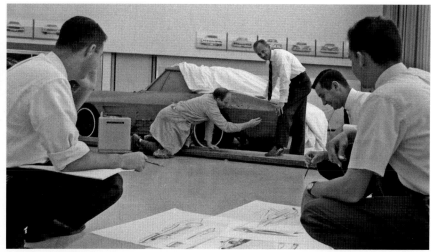

Rybicki (left with Mitchell, standing at right) was the corporate choice for succeeding Mitchell. Below is one of Rybicki's conceptual drawings.

were dictating the height and location of bumpers and lights.

General Motors also created problems for itself. Body production was moving from Fisher Body to the General Motors Assembly division. GM project centers took authority away from divisions. And in 1984 the traditional divisions were eliminated with the creation of Chevrolet-Pontiac-Canada (BPC) and Buick-Oldsmobile-Cadillac (BOC).

Perhaps the biggest challenge to design was a decision that all five GM car brands would share sheet metal. Brand identity was limited to the front and rear of the car, while the hood, roof, doors, fenders and trunk lid were shared. Cost accountants ruled the industry. And there was a vision problem. General Motors failed to see the enormity of the changes in the industry.

The 1979 Buick Riviera is one of the most successfully downsized GM designs. The 1984 Pontiac Fiero is an excellent design and the new C4 Corvette was the first in 16 years. But the worst example of these difficult times may be the unsuccessful 1982 Cadillac Cimarron. A Cadillac grille, taillights and interior were forced on the J-body structure—essentially a Chevrolet Cavalier. As Bill Mitchell said, "It's hard to tailor a dwarf."

for General Motors in 1977. GM Chairman Thomas Murphy told him, "The Mitchell era of self-aggrandizement, the non-accountability and Mitchell's blatant disregard for what the divisions wanted . . . was over. Design Staff would be run like a business."

Rybicki was a corporate choice and General Motors produced corporate cars during his design

era, which Holls and Lamm lamented as, "The darkest, bleakest period in GM design history." But the fault wasn't entirely with Rybicki.

The government required an average of 27 mpg for every vehicle a manufacturer built. One of the few solutions for a full-line manufacturer like GM was to "downsize" their cars. Other government regulations

Left: Rybicki (far right) hosts President Ronald Reagan in the studios. Right: 1979 Buick Riviera. Below: Chuck Jordan.

CHUCK JORDAN 1986–1992

Chuck Jordan was clearly Bill Mitchell's favorite, and the most like Mitchell. His career developed under Mitchell's wing. Jordan started in GM's experimental studio for trucks and progressed to responsibility for a new heavy-duty vehicles studio, where he designed earth moving equipment and railroad locomotives. But Mitchell pointed out that he would need car styling to move up at General Motors. By 1956 Jordan had his own advanced automotive studio and in 1958 he became head of the Cadillac Studio, GM's most prestigious, where he oversaw the finalization of the1959 Cadillacs.

Jordan was one of the first U.S. GM designers Mitchell sent to Opel in Germany, where his team completed the Opel GT and redesigned the Opel line with great success.

In the U.S. Bill Mitchell had chosen Chuck Jordan as his design director. Jordan made Irv Rybicki his assistant when proliferation of new GM models expanded the responsibilities of the job. One month

after becoming vice president of design in 1977, Rybicki chose Jordan as his design director. Now Jordan worked directly for Rybicki.

Dave Holls described the two men as being as different as it was possible to be. When asked how Irv Rybicki and Chuck Jordan worked together, one designer replied, "They didn't.".

GM management chose Rybicki as an admin-

istrator, however, and that gave Jordan increasing influence over design. It was Jordan who took initiatives during these difficult years. "Chuck ultimately received credit for enormous energy and total commitment. He would champion originality and creativity far more than Rybicki," wrote Holls and Lamm.

"When I took over," said Jordan in a 2006 interview, "I got everyone together that same day and I talked to them about what we were doing, and where we were going. We were going to bring back the excitement in design. And I told them we were going to have fun."

Jordan saw the opportunity to re-establish General Motors' design leadership. Working with Dave Holls' advanced studios, they created a series of concept cars for Chevrolet, Oldsmobile, Cadillac, Buick and Pontiac, including the Corvette Indy, Oldsmobile Aerotech and Buick Wildcat. The first of these were shown at GM's 1987 Teamwork & Technology exhibit, intended to make a positive statement to the financial community.

The same creativity found its way into production cars developed during Jordan's years. The 1992 Cadillac STS was introduced at the Frankfurt auto show in Germany. Jordan recalls Bruno Sacco, chief

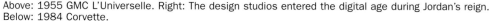

Above: 1955 GMC L'Universelle. Right: The design studios entered the digital age during Jordan's reign. Below: 1984 Corvette.

designer of Mercedes-Benz, saying to him, "I really like that car." The car that became the Oldsmobile Aurora was developed in secrecy in one of the advanced studios and displayed unexpectedly in the hallway of the Tech Center before Oldsmobile asked to build the car.

Jordan initiated early exploration of digital technology at General Motors with a "studio of tomorrow." He also worked with MIT to create a revolutionary design tool that would allow designers to display and walk around holographic images.

"I really believed we had the most talented design staff in the world," said Jordan. "If you don't have good designers, you don't have anything."

He is uniquely qualified to offer that opinion. Chuck Jordan is the only vice president of design at General Motors who worked with Harley Earl, Bill Mitchell, Irv Rybicki, Wayne Cherry and Ed Welburn. And he has always taken an interest in design education. In retirement in California, he teaches design five days a week at a local high school.

WAYNE CHERRY 1992–2003

W ayne Cherry worked with GM subsidiaries Vauxhall and Opel for 26 years before succeeding Chuck Jordan in 1992, to become the first vice president of design at General Motors who had spent most of his career in Europe.

His early years were all-American. Cherry was born in Indianapolis and attended the Indianapolis 500 every year with his father. After high school he built a 1955 Chevrolet hot rod and drove it to California when he enrolled in the Art Center School of Design.

Wayne Cherry with Mark Hogan (above). Below: Hummer H2.

Cherry and the Cadillac CTS.

He was single in 1965 and saw an assignment to Vauxhall in England as a way to see racing in Europe. At Vauxhall, he enjoyed significantly more responsibility than he would have in the U.S. He worked on "cars, trucks, military vehicles, buses, taxis, airport support vehicles, race and rally cars and race trans-

porters". His work was also gaining critical acclaim; especially the XVR and Equus show cars.

He became head of GM Design in Europe and worked with Jack Smith and Bob Lutz. They oversaw a complete overhaul of the Opel range that took the brand from last to first in European sales and

became GM's most profitable division.

When he returned to the U.S. Cherry brought a fresh perspective, and respect. As vice president of design he quickly embarked on a remarkable period of design innovation. Cherry eagerly expanded the math-based initiative started by Chuck Jordan and oversaw a $42 million installation of digital design tools that linked designers, sculptors and engineers.

Cherry re-established advanced design studios. He placed renewed emphasis on individual brand character. Twenty-seven individual GM design studios were replaced with eight brand character studios and a corporate brand center was created, where multidisciplinary teams match brand "DNA" and ideas with brand studios. The brand center also pioneered the use of foam models, which could be created

Hummer H2, Pontiac Solstice, the redesigned Cadillac line and both the C5 and C6 Corvettes were designed in Cherry's studios. A total of 40 concept cars were created between just 1999 and early 2004, the most in any GM design era. Of these, he believes the most significant was the Cadillac Sixteen of 2003.

Above and right: Pontiac Solstice concepts. Below: Cadillac's Sixteen.

and modified faster and less-expensively than clay models.

He was reunited with Jack Smith as president of General Motors, and with Bob Lutz who rejoined GM from retirement in 2001 to lead product development and established an order where engineering, manufacturing and design all reported to him.

Creativity soared in the new environment. The

Cherry also recognized the importance of developing a strong design team with diverse experiences and global perspective. In addition to Ed Welburn, who had spent his career at General Motors, he brought top designers into GM from other companies, including Audi, Volkswagen, Renault and Daimler-Benz as well as Vauxhall and Opel.

Wayne Cherry's legacy will also include stewardship of the restoration of Harley Earl's Design Center prior to the 75th Anniversary of General Motors Design in 2003. In addition to subtly introducing state-of-the-art technology into the facility, many features were restored to their original finish or replicated, including the "tea cup" reception desk in the lobby.

ED WELBURN 2003–

Quipped Ed Welburn, "We should be doing this in my office. The same office where Harley Earl—all of us—have worked." Instead the conversation was taking place at the 2006 New York Auto Show. The setting was as auspicious, where current and future GM designs were displayed in an environment alongside their competitors.

The transformation of Cadillac, always General Motors' design leader, was complete. The brand character of Chevrolet and Pontiac—platform twins for decades—had been reasserted dramatically. Buick's Lucerne was being compared favorably with the quality of the world's best automakers. The Hummer had become an icon of GM design and Oldsmobile, with over 100 years of heritage, was gone.

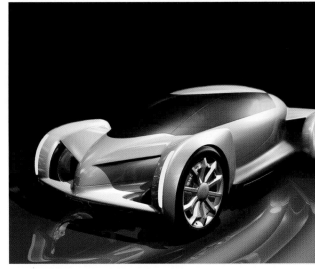

The AUTOnomy concept.

Ed Welburn presides over GM Design in a world very different from Harley Earl's. Markets and design are global. It is no longer enough to lead the American automobile industry. To succeed—even to survive, some would say—General Motors must reassert global leadership.

This was evidenced by the revival of GM's Saturn brand at the New York show. Three new models and the PreVue concept were introduced in New York. Welburn stood in the center of all four vehicles and pointed out the strong character that unites them and the unmistakable influence of GM's European Design Center at Opel in Russelsheim, Germany.

The Oldmobile Aerotech.

It had been announced just days earlier that future Saturn products would be based on Opel designs.

"For me, many things have changed but others have not," said Welburn. "We have returned to our roots."

Ed Welburn's roots at GM are deep. He started designing cars early, drawing on the pages of his mother's books. A photograph shows him as a GM summer intern shaking hands with Bill Mitchell, then-VP of design. He joined GM full time in 1972, working in advanced studios for Oldsmobile and Buick before being assigned to the Buick production studio. He later worked in Dave Holl's advanced studio where he was largely responsible for the design of the Oldsmobile Aerotech. In addition to being exhibited as part of GM's Teamwork & Technology, the Aerotech set a closed-course speed record of over 278 mph with A.J Foyt driving.

Above: Production on the much-anticipated next-generation Camaro will begin at the end of 2008. Its concept was developed in GM's high-tech studios, now overseen by Welburn.

Another design Welburn considers most significant is the AUTOnomy concept, showcasing hydrogen fuel technology in a unique "skateboard" chassis with interchangeable bodies. Shades of Harley Earl's Firebird turbine cars.

Today he presides over a GM Design organization that includes Russelsheim, studios in England, Brazil, Australia, Korea, China and California. But the Design Center in Warren, Michigan is still at the center. "When our designers from around the world come through those gates," he said, "It's like Mecca."

Or Camelot. **AQ**

Art Gallery with
John Francis Marsh

Before he and the Lusitania both were drowned in the Irish Sea, author and publisher Elbert Hubbard was among America's top producers of pithy, sensible sayings. To wit, his definition of the word "editor": "A person employed by a newspaper whose business it is to separate the wheat from the chaff, and to see that the chaff is printed."

Without labeling either as wheat or chaff, Hubbard saw a similar divide between art and science: "Art is the beautiful way of doing things. Science is the effective way of doing things."

One wonders what Hubbard would make of the paintings of John Francis Marsh, which, like the man himself, are both artful and

> **"There's a science to making a painting," Marsh said. "It's no different from building a computer or a hair dryer or a packaging system"**

"America: Bold, Confident and Free."
Watercolor, 30 x 40 inches

BY GERRY DURNELL

technical. In Marsh's work, logic and magic are partners, not competitors. In one 30-second segment, his conversation touches on his appreciation for each element's contribution to creating something that is beautiful and effective at the same time.

"There's a science to making a painting," Marsh said. "It's no different from building a computer or a hair dryer or a packaging system.

"But there's nothing magic about that board until I start putting the magic on it. When I put the magic on it, that board becomes a visual circus of events for the eye."

Small wonder that Marsh blends calculation and imagination so effortlessly. Before he started painting automobiles, he worked as a product designer for General Motors. The best industrial designers strive to maximize form and function alike. The ideal result

Opposite: "Scaglietti Suite."
Watercolor, 12 x 18 inches.

Marsh, at home at his easel in West Point, California.

is a product that looks as good as it works, and works as good as it looks.

Marsh is renowned for his paintings of automobiles that accomplish both goals. One of his favorite and most famous works is "Concept 1," which was commissioned by Volkswagen of America in 1993 to commemorate the reinvention of the iconic Beetle.

The painting not only celebrates the Bug's sleek, new look but the hard work that went into creating it. The car is surrounded by humans—designers, draftsmen and engineers—engaged in various stages of taking the modern Beetle from idea to reality.

"Concept 1" is a pluperfect example of Marsh's

"I want to keep the eye attracted to the painting. People could stand in front of the board for hours, if they had the time, and never get bored with it."

ability to turn an intricately planned array of images into a vibrant composition that does indeed put magic on the board.

"I want to keep the eye attracted to the painting," he said. "People could stand in front of the bo hours, if they had the time, and never get bored with it."

Above: "Fast, Small, Personal and America." Watercolor, 30 x 40 inches. Below: From 1996, the watercolor, "Brothers of Destiny".

Towards the end of the second semester, the school found out that he was about to leave in an effort to earn more money to continue his education there. That was deemed unacceptable, so Art Center decided to award the first full scholarship to a freshman student. Marsh said he will always be grateful to the Libby Owens Ford Corporation, which funded the last three years of his education. He earned a Bachelor's of Professional Arts degree, graduating with honors.

Marsh graduated from Art Center in 1959 and started a career in industrial design, working first for GM as a product designer. After working for GM for two years on a variety of special and interesting design projects, he left to work as a full-time product

Marsh, 68, has been entertaining people with his art since he was a kindergartener drawing World War II airplanes. By the time he reached high school, Marsh was a genuine prodigy. He won four General Motors Fisher Body Craftsman Guild awards while at Wilcox Technical School in Meriden, Conn. He graduated with the second-highest grade-point average in school history.

Marsh also was awarded scholarships to Carnegie Tech, University of Bridgeport's Industrial Design School, Hartford Art School and Yale Design School. To the dismay of his teachers and parents, he accepted the scholarship to Bridgeport.

His dream was to attend the Art Center School in Los Angeles, and attending Bridgeport allowed him an opportunity to save enough money to do just that. After his year at Bridgeport, Marsh was accepted to his dream school and had saved enough money to put him through two semesters.

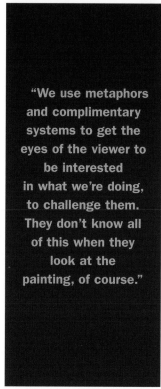

Part two of the "Lincoln Heritage Triptych" titled "Continental Years." Watercolor, 30 x 40 inches.

designer for Sundburg and Ferar Industrial design in Southfield, Mich., before leaving to start his own industrial design firm in San Francisco, called Hisata, Ishimaru, Montgomery and Marsh.

The first automobile Marsh owned he purchased while still with GM. Car 1 foreshadowed "Concept 1."

"It was a silver 1958 VW," Marsh said. "It had belonged to a GM executive. They'd been told to park the thing in the very back of the GM lot."

In 1972, Marsh quit the workaday world in order to paint full time. His early work focused on landscapes and portraits. Marsh didn't turn his attention to automobiles and shop scenes until 1989, when his former Art Center instructor and mentor, Strother MacMinn,

suggested he try painting his now-famous Talbot Lago shop scene called "Two for Le Mans."

Though Marsh appreciates race cars, he feels no need for speed. In fact, he still regards the motorcycle ride he took on the back of a BSA (Birmingham Small Arms Co.) Gold Star in 1955 as "the most terrifying moment of my life."

"I'm not interested in thrills, spills and chills," Marsh said. "All of those words end in 'ills,' you know."

Marsh drives a Toyota 4Runner around his West Point, Calif., home and uses a 1971 Toyota Land Cruiser to do the dirty work on his Sierra Nevada ranch. He is happiest putting his vehicles in park and working in his 600-square-foot studio, complete with

a library and basement.

"I'm a morning person," he said. "And if I'm really chopping away, I'll keep going until 10 o'clock at night."

Marsh used to chop away at 50 paintings a year. He does fewer but much larger pieces these days, 30-by-40s mostly.

"I'm much more interested in the grand painting now," Marsh said. "There's more challenge to it. When you get a board that big, you have to make sure everything is working—all of the sub-compositions.

"We use metaphors and complimentary systems to get the eyes of the viewer to be interested in what we're doing, to challenge them. They don't know all

the point where the art mixes with the moneybag—and that's important."

John and his wife Patty Kris make their home at Stonehaven in the Sierras. John built the home in the early 1970s, out of the stone found on the land, which is how it earned its name. When the weather gets too cold or too hot they escape to their home Shorehaven in Pacific Grove, on the Monterey Peninsula. ◭◳

Left: Part three of the "Lincoln Heritage Triptych titled "LA Steamrollers." Below "Winds of Change." Watercolor, 20 x 30 inches.

of this when they look at the painting, of course."

Marsh is currently working on a large portrait of Ed Gilbertson and Sherry Lindberg, the well-known contest judges who recently retired from the Ferrari Club of America. Club members commissioned Marsh to paint whatever the couple wanted. They chose to be pictured sitting in an early Ferrari Barchetta, surrounded by paintings and models of other rare cars they have owned, along with some of their vintage motorcycles.

Much of Marsh's time doesn't involve painting at all. The former star student is now an enthusiastic instructor for the Academy of Art University in San Francisco. He teaches Design Drawing 2 and the History of Industrial Design.

Marsh is delighted by the opportunity to share his hard-won knowledge, along with his conviction

that the designers of today will profoundly influence the world of tomorrow.

"I have found it very rewarding because I get to see my students grow up and really develop as industrial designers," Marsh said. "Because that was my field and what my expertise and degrees are in, it is kind of nice to see that you can influence some young people who will be very instrumental in changing the way the world lives in the future. The industrial design profession is at

"VW Concept 1" All of the people seen in this Concept 1 shop scene actually worked on the Concept 1. When Marsh creates a shop scene, he makes it as realistic as possible always using the actual people doing their jobs. Watercolor, 19 x 29 inches.

ABBEY

MISTER LISTER

ROAD TO LE MANS
The Lister Story

1956 Lister-Bristol leads 1958 Lister-Chevy in a road race.

For six glorious years great sports-racing cars emerged from a general engineering shop in England's Cambridge. The saga of their rise and fall and their astonishing successes is as dramatic as any in the history of motor sports.

BY KARL LUDVIGSEN

It would be hard to say which was more competitive in the 1950s—big-bore sports-car racing in Britain or America. In both countries the top stables and drivers relished the punch and potency of the fastest sports machinery, be it Allard, Ferrari, Maserati or Jaguar. Toward the latter part of the decade, however, a new name appeared among the winners of the most prestigious national races. Lister became the name with which to conjure. Britain's Lister was the marque toward which the best men and teams gravitated as if impelled by sheer magnetism.

The motive for their Listermania was the electrifying racing record of one Jaguar-powered car in 1957. "Without any doubt," wrote Briton John Bolster, "the most outstanding feature of the 1957 racing season in this country has been Archie Scott-Brown's mastery of the sports-car events with the Lister-Jaguar."

The factory's first Lister-Jaguar entered 14 races and won 11. At every track in either practice or the race it either equaled or broke the lap record. And it did so against stiff competition from Jaguar D-Types and factory Aston Martins. The latter in particular were deeply annoyed that this brash newcomer, with a budget for its whole season costing no more than a couple of Aston Martin crankshafts, could so decisively defeat their finely tooled machines.

Lister's venture into the big leagues was impeccably timed. The seeds of its success were planted in October of 1956. In that month Jaguar announced that "after very serious consideration" it was suspending the works-backed racing activities that had seen its cars dominating the winner's circle at Le Mans from 1952 through 1956. It was time, Jaguar said, to concentrate on its future production cars. But the fevered pulse of Jaguar's racing enthusiasts wouldn't be slowed that easily.

Above: Lister with his much-modified Morgan 4/4 in April 1950. Right: Brian Lister competing in a Cambridge club sprint event in his Morgan 4/4 in March 1950.

That same month Brian Horace Lister, the man behind his eponymous racing cars, came to London for his regular visit with Brian Turle. The latter, who held the purse strings of British Petroleum's

motor-racing sponsorship, had already backed Lister's efforts for several seasons. Brian Lister was eager to know whether BP would support his idea of building single-seaters for the new 1.5-liter Formula 2, which would kick off on 1957. In fact he was already building a suitable car.

Turle rocked Lister back on his heels. "We want you to build a big sports car with a Jaguar engine," he told the Cambridge businessman. The BP executive had his reasons. The main opposition to Jaguar in British racing was Aston Martin, which was backed by Esso. Jaguar wanted marketplace rival Aston kept in its place even after it left the field. Scotland's Ecurie Ecosse was racing Jaguars, but it too was Esso-aided. Turle saw Lister as the man to move up a class to challenge these opponents. By coincidence, Lister's green and yellow racing colors were similar to those of BP.

At first sight this was a tall order. Hitherto Lister had built 19 sports-racing cars, all with engines of 2.0 liters or smaller. Installing a 3.5-liter Jaguar that

produced twice the horsepower and weighed half again as much would be no walk in the park. One of Lister's customers had asked for a Jaguar installation which Brian had agreed to carry out only because he didn't want to see someone else make a hash of it.

Lister told Turle he'd think about it and returned the 65 miles north to home base at Cambridge, where George Lister & Sons Ltd. was on the university town's east side, just a stone's throw from the River Cam in the midst of a terrace of Victorian houses. Since the retirement of their father Horace in 1954, Brian and his brother Raymond were the joint managing directors of a company renowned in

Above: Lister's first serious competition car was this MG-powered Cooper, here with its top and windscreen in place. Right: Lister in a club sprint event with his Cooper-MG. Unhappy with the car, he looked for a better solution. Left: Meeting John Tojeiro, Lister commissioned his second chassis and installed a vee-twin JAP air-cooled engine of 1.1 liters. He asked Archie Scott-Brown to drive it.

the region for its metalworking skills. A 40-strong staff and versatile machine tools were capable of wrought-iron work and general fabrication of high quality that sustained the firm since its founding in 1890 by Brian's grand-dad in the back garden of his house.

As was his style, Brian Lister talked the idea over with his colleagues. One of the closest was Don

Above: The first Lister car, MG-powered BHL 1, in chassis form and at the Prescott Hillclimb in 1954 with Jack Sears driving. Right: The first Lister-Bristol winning the race for 2-liter sports cars at the International Trophy Meeting, August 1954, Archie Scott-Brown at the wheel.

Moore, who'd done some racing before concentrating on engine preparation. Moore's skills and his Cambridge facilities were an integral part of Lister's successes. "I think that could be quite a good idea," was Moore's reaction. "You never know, you might be able to get some of the Americans—a chap like Briggs Cunningham—interested in something like that." This made sense to the commercially astute Lister. "I went back to Turle," said Lister, "and told him yes, we'd do it."

Both Turle and Lister were well aware that the car builder possessed a valuable asset over and above his self-taught engineering skills. The most striking successes his cars had hitherto achieved were to the credit of a Glasgow-born driver, William Archibald Scott-Brown. Born in 1927, a year after Brian Lister, Archie Scott-Brown was handsome, mustachioed and passionate about cars. Having spent much of his inheritance on an MG TD, in 1951 he began driving it in the sprint events of the Cambridge University Automobile Club.

Also competing in the Club's events was Brian Lister. "I went to the Perse School in Cambridge,"

Lister recalled. "But I wasn't very interested in what they were teaching me and I left at 15. My father, who was interested in me becoming a practical businessman, said, 'You'd better come and learn your trade.' I was apprenticed as a fitter machinist and welder. After my apprenticeship in July of 1945 I enlisted in the RAF as a flight mechanic for my military service for a couple of years.

"I was getting more and more interested in motor

cars," Lister continued, "reading books by people like Prince Bira and Chula. Of course I couldn't get very interested in them during the war because you couldn't get any petrol. When I got back I started modifying the car that I had at the time, which was a Climax-engined Morgan 4/4, lightening it and gradually getting more interested in motor sports. Previously I'd been more interested in jazz music and playing in jazz groups."

Left: Archie Scott-Brown won the contest at Brands Hatch for unlimited sports cars, May 29, 1955, in the Lister-Bristol. Right: The Lister-Bristol of 1955 with new Thom Lucas bodywork, here unpainted. This was the car of Ormsby Issard-Davies, driven by Alan Moore at Oulton Park in 1955. Below: On left in front of the Lister offices the hugely successful works Lister-Bristol of 1954-55, next to the new Maserati-engined "Flat-iron" of 1956.

It dawned on Lister that his new enthusiasm had a certain congruence with the family business: "I came to the conclusion that I could possibly get some free publicity for the company, which would help with the engineering business, and ordered a sports-car chassis from John Cooper in which I fitted an MG engine. I ran a few races and sprints with it with reasonable success. Then a fellow came in to see me and wanted some parts made for a car that he was building. That was John Tojeiro."

A graduate of the Perse School a few years ahead of Lister, Tojeiro was at the beginning of a distinguished career as a competition-car designer and builder that would include his creation of the AC Cobra chassis. Unhappy with his Cooper-MG, Lister commissioned John Tojeiro's second-ever racer. "I put a JAP air-cooled dirt-track twin in it, coupled up to a Jowett Jupiter gearbox, and got it running, but it was so quick that it rather put the wind up me!" In a time trial Lister saw a much heavier and less powerful MG TD clocking only half a second over his time in the light, potent Tojeiro-JAP. Wheels began to turn.

"I came to the conclusion that he would probably drive a bit better than I would," Lister reflected. "The whole idea was to promote the engineering company, with local races and sprints, so I offered him the ride. And that was Archie Scott-Brown. In 1953 he was competing in the 1,100 sports-car class, and admittedly there wasn't very much competition, but while the engine lasted he won every race. That was quite a successful start in our relationship."

Those meeting the charming Archie Scott-Brown noted that he was on the short side, just over five feet, and walked with a limp. While some assumed that he'd been wounded in the recent war, in fact he was seriously handicapped. Bones were missing in his legs, feet were malformed and the right arm was stunted below the elbow. But behind the wheel he was a demon with an uncanny sense of balance and total car control. "He was so quick," said Lister, "that when he was backing the Tojeiro out of my barn he turned the steering wheel so quickly that its spokes blurred."

to design my own car and get Archie to drive it," he recalled, "because I thought that we could do a bit of good." His lack of high-flown technical qualifications didn't daunt him: "I read technical articles in *The Motor* and *The Autocar*, bought and read books and looked at motor cars."

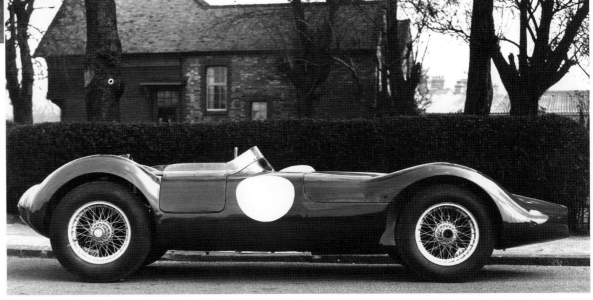

Left: Fabricating the low-line Lister-Maserati for 1956, using components of the original MG-engined Lister, in the Abbey Road workshop. Right: The Lister-Maserati, showing ducting to carburetors from cowl-mounted air intake and extra duct at front to oil cooler. Disc brakes were now fitted. Below: The spectacular finished design would inspire the first Lister-Jaguar of 1957.

As he moved up in class Scott-Brown's handicap led to controversy over his fitness to race a car. He would have to wait out several "medical" inquests into his capability and continental race organizers would never fully accept him. In light of this he was grateful to Brian Lister for his early and unstinting support and encouragement. The two men forged a personal partnership that remained informal; they had no contract. But although Scott-Brown would race for other teams, including Connaught in Formula 1, Lister would always have first call on his services as Bryan Turle was well aware.

Having found a superb driver on home ground, Brian Lister proceeded determined on a step that would have daunted many. "I decided that I ought

Having the idea was one thing but financing it was another, said Lister: "I put the plan to my father, who was still managing director of the family company. He said, 'Right, what's it going to cost?' I said, 'I don't really know, but I don't think you're going to see much change out of 1,500 or 2,000 pounds.' So he said, 'I'll give you 1,500 and six months. If you haven't had any success in that time, you can forget the whole thing.' I took the challenge on. I had a close look at what was around and what was successful, and started from there. I started designing the car in the summer of 1953."

Lister spaced 5.50 x 16 wheels on a compact 90-inch wheelbase with 49.8-inch track front and rear. MG hubs and uprights at front were carried by tubular parallel wishbones of Brian's own design, sprung from well-braced towers by concentric coil springs and shock absorbers. The ubiquitous Morris Minor rack-and-pinion steering gear was mounted in front of the suspension.

Joining front and rear was a twin-tube frame that was widest at the front of the seats, tapering in again at the rear. The tubes were 3.0-inch diameter with 16-gauge walls. Towers at the rear held similar springing media above the hubs of a de Dion tube

Above left: Archie Scott-Brown in the Lister-Maserati at Aintree, June 23, 1956, for the international meeting. He won the 2-liter class and placed fourth overall in the unlimited sports-car race. Above right: Brown in the Lister-Maserati's first appearance at Oulton Park on April 14, 1956, in the BRDC Empire Trophy races. Here he placed second in his heat but overheated in the main race. Right: The stunning lines of the Lister-Maserati are evident in this shot of Scott Brown, again at Oulton Park on Aug. 18, 1956.

curving around behind a frame-mounted Salisbury differential. Ambitiously, to reduce unsprung weight Lister mounted the rear brakes inboard, next to the differential. Here, as in the location of the de Dion axle by twin radius rods and a sliding block at the center, were signs of influence by the design of the successful HWM Formula 2 car of 1952-53.

Compared to the HWM, Brian Lister was more advanced in his use of concentric coil springs and dampers, a relatively new notion. Although disc brakes were just beginning to be seen, he felt that Girling's shoe brakes in finned Al-Fin drums would be enough to stop a light sports car with its Moore-prepared 1.5-liter MG engine.

"We had a rolling chassis by Christmas of 1953," Lister recalled. Early in '54 he and Archie took the chassis to the airport circuit at Snetterton. Fifty miles to the northeast in Norfolk, this was their home track for baptisms of Lister cars. Thereafter the chassis went to Byfleet, near the old Brooklands track, to be bodied by Wakefields to Brian's straightforward full-envelope design. The front of its aluminum skin lifted up for engine access in the manner of the C-Type Jaguar. Wakefields charged £275 for the work, absorbing almost one-fifth of Lister's total budget.

Brian Lister had one last design job. A new car

Above left: Under the hood of a 1956 "Flat-iron" Lister-Bristol, showing the height of the Bristol six with its triple-downdraft carbs. Above right: "Flat-iron" Lister-Bristols in action at Aintree, June 23, 1956. Alan Moore, who placed third in class, leads Noel Cunningham-Reid. Left: Engine expert Don Moore—here with a Bristol cylinder head—prepared Lister's racing engines and contributed greatly to the works team's success.

marque needed a suitable badge. "The obvious thing to start with is a circle because that's the most elegant geometric form," he related. "I thought I'd divide it up into three or four, but I couldn't get much inspiration so I started looking through a book that my father bought me when I was about six or seven years old, a kind of illustrated encyclopaedia of everything. Looking through it I came across the Boy Scout merit badges. The Messenger was a geometric design like three scimitars equally distributed round a circle. That's quite a nice design, I thought. I think I'll produce something like that. All the way through motor racing that's what we used."

In April 1954 the first Lister was ready to race, given serial number BHL 1 using Brian's initials. Controversy over Scott-Brown's handicap kept him out of its cockpit for a few races; Ken Wharton and Jack Sears stepped in to show that the little car had winning potential. In its class, however, the light-weight Lotus was even quicker, so Brian went back to father Horace for funding for Plan B: the building of a second car powered by Bristol's lively six-cylinder engine, patterned on the pre-war BMW 328.

Given the go-ahead, the Lister workshops quickly produced BHL 2 with track increased to 50 inches

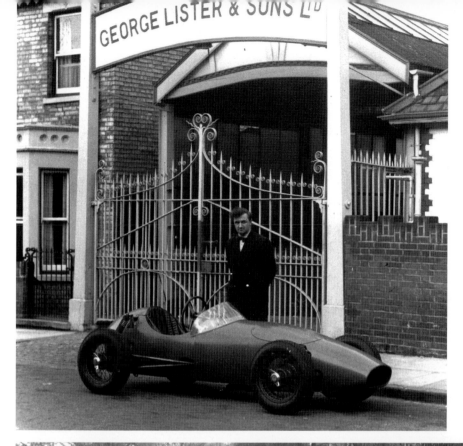

Left: Lister posed next to his first Formula 2 car outside the works entrance to George Lister & Sons. This car would be set aside before competing. Right: In 1957, Lister had another attempt at a Formula 2 car design, inclining the Coventry Climax four to achieve a low line. Below: The 1957 Lister-Jaguar with Scott Brown in the car and Lister standing. This car would win 11 times in 14 tries.

and brake diameter raised from 9 to 11 inches. A bulge in the front deck made room for the much taller engine. With Don Moore's 142 bhp from the Bristol in 1,350 pounds of agile Lister the Cambridge team discovered the right formula. It made its debut during the year's most important meeting, the British Grand Prix on July 17, 1954. While the Lister-MG was outclassed in the supporting 1.5-liter race, Archie flew in the race for unlimited sports cars in what *The Motor* called "the extraordinary looking Lister-Bristol."

The Lister, said the weekly, "not only retained its class lead until the finish but also proceeded to do battle with the big boys, overtaking car after car to complete the race in fifth position in the general classification ahead of all the Jaguar XK120Cs." Only Aston Martins and a Lagonda were ahead of Archie—and he was only two seconds behind the Lagonda, with more than twice the displacement, after 52 minutes.

Because the main race was so important, the first British GP of the new Formula 1 with Ferrari, Maserati and Mercedes-Benz competing, the meeting was televised. Brian recalled that his father,

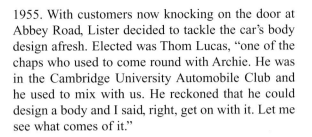

Left: This Lister-Jag of 1958, a third production "Knobbly," had magnesium bodywork (an option) and unique air vents in its flanks. Below: Utterly purposeful, the 1957 Lister-Jag, first of a new breed. During the season a large rear scoop was added to aid the rear-deck vents in cooling the brakes and differential.

1955. With customers now knocking on the door at Abbey Road, Lister decided to tackle the car's body design afresh. Elected was Thom Lucas, "one of the chaps who used to come round with Archie. He was in the Cambridge University Automobile Club and he used to mix with us. He reckoned that he could design a body and I said, right, get on with it. Let me see what comes of it."

The Lucas body, one of only two Lister models not designed by Brian himself, was a professional-looking effort, exotic by British standards with its curved-in fins, front-wheelhouse fences and long hood bulge to disguise the Bristol.

Then a Cambridge student, Lucas tested a scale model of his design in the wind tunnel of the University's engineering laboratory. Again executed by Wakefield, four Lister-Bristols to this design were sold, together with several chassis to be owner-bodied.

Best results with the customer cars in 1955 were registered by Noel Cunningham-Reid and Jack Sears, while Archie Scott-Brown carried on in his 1954 Lister-Bristol. "We continued racing that car," Lister explained, "principally because we couldn't have got an extra one out in time for the start of the season. Nor was I really convinced about the aerodynamic efficiency of the new car. Also, the cost of making an extra motor car came into the equation."

Among Archie's many 1955 successes was a notable win at Oulton Park in April's Empire Trophy

watching at home, "simply could not credit the number of times the company name was mentioned. From that moment on he thoroughly approved of my building racing cars." Young Lister also convinced an older member of his staff at Abbey Road: "He came up to me and said he'd seen a report about the Lister-Bristol in the newspaper *The News of the World*. 'You

know,' he said, 'you have to have achieved something to get reported in *The News of the World*.' I thought, bloody hell, I've made it!"

Though Bristol-powered sports-racing cars were also fielded by Kieft, Lotus, Frazer-Nash and Cooper in 1954, the Lister proved the best of the bunch. Not standing still, Brian Lister refined his car's design for

that we were the right kind of people to use their engine."

To carry the Modena-made six Lister cannibalized BHL 1, the original MG-powered chassis. It was updated throughout, including 10-inch Girling disc brakes, still inboard at the rear. The 20-gauge aluminum sheet around it, again shaped by Wakefield, was a Brian Lister masterpiece. Ultra-low with bulges over its wheels, the laden 1956 Lister was only 27 inches high at its headrest. The press called it "arresting", "very impressive" and "a speed recipe". Its nickname became "Flat-iron" after the low-line racing cars built by Parry Thomas in the 1920s. With

Above: A 1958 Lister-Jag in full flow at Goodwood. Left: The cockpit, with Lister emblem on the wheel and central shift lever for the Jaguar's four-speed box. Right: With its hood off, the special Lister-Jag that raced at Monza in 1958.

Race. In damp conditions Scott-Brown was fastest of all qualifiers—including Ferrari Monzas and D-Type Jaguars—by two seconds. He went on to place second in his heat and win the final. His Lister-Bristol scored many class successes and was the outright winner of unlimited sports-car races at Brands Hatch and Goodwood.

Unconvinced as he was about the Lucas body's aerodynamics, Brian Lister decided to have a go himself for 1956. "I don't claim to be a body designer," he explained. "As far as airflow is concerned I didn't know much about it. But my principle was that you make it as small as you can, as low as you can and as attractive as you can." His inspiration for a new shape was the MG streamliner built pre-war for Major Goldie Gardner to designs by Reid Railton.

Lister studied MG expert Don Moore's scale model of this record-breaking car.

Only one thing stood in the way of making a car "as low as you can" and that was the Bristol six, with its high-placed carburetors. "The Bristol engine was something like 29 inches tall," said Lister. He had his eye on a unit seven inches shorter, the dry-sump, twin-cam six-cylinder engine of the A6GCS/2000 Maserati that had been troublesome to the Lister-Bristol. To get one he appealed to BP, which was also backing Maserati: "BP confirmed to Maserati

its stressed nosepiece the new car weighed only 1,175 pounds.

The stunning looks of the latest Lister attracted buyers of Bristol-engined versions, who put up with substantial bulges in their Flat-irons to house their taller sixes. Buyers now dealt with Brian Lister (Light Engineering) Ltd., a separate company that Brian set up to sell and service racing cars. The example of the 1955 Le Mans disaster convinced him that he needed to have clear demarcation that would protect the main metalworking business in

One of Lister's greatest regrets was a Cunningham team failure at a pit stop that stranded this Moss/Bueb Lister-Jaguar without fuel when it was leading at Sebring in 1959. Retiring a healthy car! No greater sin in racing.

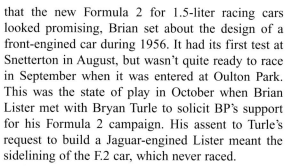

Left: A Cunningham racing Lister-Jag of 1958. Below left: Frank Costin, left, held one end of the space frame he was creating at Lister during 1959. One of the Cunningham Team's "Knobbly" Lister-Jaguars.

that the new Formula 2 for 1.5-liter racing cars looked promising, Brian set about the design of a front-engined car during 1956. It had its first test at Snetterton in August, but wasn't quite ready to race in September when it was entered at Oulton Park. This was the state of play in October when Brian Lister met with Bryan Turle to solicit BP's support for his Formula 2 campaign. His assent to Turle's request to build a Jaguar-engined Lister meant the sidelining of the F.2 car, which never raced.

Lister hadn't quite purged Formula 2 from his system. In 1957 he had another go at a front-engined car which suffered from oiling problems with its inclined twin-cam Climax engine. Near the end of that season it had a couple of indifferent outings.

case any suit were brought as a result of a car-racing tragedy. Records indicate that seven of the Bristol-powered cars, with exhaust-pipe niches on the right rather than the left, left Abbey Road in 1956.

Hopes were high for the works of Lister-Maserati with its Moore-tuned engine, capable of 170 bhp. "It went reasonably well while it was going," said Lister of his new creation, "but it was the most unreliable thing I think we ever got involved with. We had constant trouble with various things."

Engine troubles kept Scott-Brown from starring again in the Empire Trophy at Oulton Park. In August the Maserati behaved at Brands Hatch, where Archie won both the unlimited sports-car race and the Formula Libre race in a Connaught. He had several class wins as well, but it was evident during 1956 that in the smaller categories the latest designs from Lotus and Cooper—the latter mid-engined—were becoming troublesome.

What was to be the next step for Lister? Deciding

"As soon as the Lister-Jaguar took off the way it did I discarded it," said *Le Patron*. "I don't think it would have been successful but I wasn't going to give it a chance to be unsuccessful."

Lister had another reason for discarding his Formula-car initiative. Pressing it would have absorbed too much of the resources of George Lister & Sons Ltd. "What I didn't want to do was to ruin the core business by getting too involved in motor racing," Lister recalled. The main business in fact was flourishing thanks to the publicity given Lister's successes.

The all-conquering Lister-Jaguar of 1957 was patterned closely in looks and technology after the Maserati-engined Flat-iron, proving again the adage that there's no better way to build a good big car than to develop it from a good small car. Wheelbase and track were little changed while the frame-tube gauge was increased from 16 to 14. A low hood line was still possible thanks to the dry-sump layout of the 3.5-liter racing D-Type six supplied by Jaguar for one-third the cost of the Maserati engine. Curb weight was 1,740 pounds distributed 48 percent-52 percent front to rear.

The result was a sleek green and yellow missile of a sports-racer with brake-cooling ducts flanking its radiator-air inlet. Vents—and later a scoop—were added to its rear deck for cooling. During '57 Jaguar supplied a 3.8-liter version of its six. In this form a test by John Bolster in *Autosport* recorded acceleration to 60 mph in 4.6 seconds—in first gear—and to 100 in 11.2 seconds. It took 13.2 seconds to cover the standing quarter-mile, reaching 110 mph at the end. Bolster attributed to it "a most stirring getaway" and "immense acceleration".

Bolster's test was part of a Lister public-relations operation in the autumn of 1957 that also saw *The*

Left: The Costin-bodied Lister-Jaguar of 1959. Right: First of the new Costin-bodied Listers, more rounded and voluminous to reduce drag. Below: This was one of two Ford V8-powered Sunbeam Tigers built by Lister for Le Mans in 1964. With Lister not responsible for their entry, they retired with engine maladies.

Autocar take the sports-racer on the road for a three-day drive. Brian Lister was soliciting customers for a production run of Jaguar-powered cars for 1958. In international sports-car championship events they'd have to have 3.0-liter engines—a new rule for '58—but they could continue to use 3.8-liter sixes in British and American national events.

The car that started it all, the ludicrously successful '57 Lister-Jaguar, went to New Zealand in the early months of 1958 to compete in Formula Libre races, two of which Scott-Brown won outright. After its return it was broken up to save space in the factory. "That was the one that won all the races and it was the one that I stupidly cut up—threw away," rued Brian Lister. "The biggest bloody mistake I ever made."

Lister had no time to dwell on the future market for historic sports-racers because his works was bursting at the seams to build 1958 Listers. In August Brian received a phone call from Lofty England, formerly Jaguar's racing manager and now its service director. Briggs Cunningham was coming over, said England. Could Lister receive him and his entourage? Briggs Cunningham! Don Moore's forecast had been right on the money.

Having stopped building his own cars after 1955, Cunningham became a Jaguar distributor and enthusiastic entrant and occasional driver of its D-Types in American racing. With the opposition intensifying, however, and Jaguar no longer developing new cars, the Lister looked interesting. Briggs visited England in September of 1957 with technical chief Alfred Momo and ace driver Walt Hansgen in tow.

The '57 Lister-Jaguar was trailered out to Snetterton and turned loose in the hands of Scott Brown and Hansgen. Walt liked the car very much—particularly its high cornering speed and the de Dion rear's traction—and posted a time just a second longer than Archie's best for the course. Cunningham placed an order for three cars, two to accommodate a Jaguar engine and the other to suit the Chevrolet V8, which was starting to come into its own as a racing engine.

With Cunningham as bell cow, others in America jumped to sign up as Lister buyers, racers and distributors: Tom Carstens in Tacoma, Washington; Carroll Shelby in Dallas, Texas and Lindy Hansen's Auto Engineering in Lexington, Mass. Carstens, the wealthy Kelso Auto-dynamics team and Texas's Jim Hall were among those most interested in the Chevy engines, while European teams like Ecurie Ecosse and Ecurie Nationale Belge preferred Jaguar power.

The successful twin-tube frame design was retained for the new cars. Using Girling tubular dampers, the rear coil springs were increased in diameter and leaned inward more sharply to decrease the height of the tail section, where the spare wheel was now under the fuel tank—reversing the 1957 positions.

Introduced in 1957, new FIA rules specified a mandatory full-width windscreen height. Puzzling over the reconciliation of this with the lowest possible frontal area, Brian Lister hit on the idea of

Above: Works 3.0-liter Lister-Jag of Bueb/Halford at Le Mans 1959. It was fourth at one-third distance but retired thereafter.

submerging the cowl—and thus the base of the windscreen—several inches below the top of the bulge over the Jaguar six. Then he aligned the top of the rear deck with the top of the screen. The bodies were made at Edmonton in North London by Williams & Pritchard.

With bulges over the wheels, the new car's DNA was clearly that of the Lister-Maserati. Exhaust piping was now enclosed in the rocker panel, which was heavily louvered by Alfred Momo. The result was an awesome-looking car that deserved its "Knobbly" nickname. In fact the abrupt curvature of its front fenders was found to generate lift, which Ecurie Ecosse reduced by fairing the fenders more gradually to the rear.

Beefing up the '57 design created a 1958 Lister-Jaguar which, at 1,920 pounds, was only a smidgen lighter than a D-Type. Cunningham had hoped for better, but the new car's advantages of low build and

outstanding drive traction—helped by a Dana limited-slip differential—were convincing. Walt Hansgen cut a swathe through SCCA National racing in 1958, taking the Class C Modified championship with Ed Crawford second in another Lister-Jaguar.

Early problems with the new model in Europe were caused by the increased grip of Dunlop's new R5 tire as fed back through the steering. First to suffer were the steering-rack mountings. After these were strengthened the steering arms wilted—not a good problem to have. The needed improvements were quickly communicated by Brian Lister to his customers, who much appreciated his solicitude.

To his astonishment and dismay Archie Scott-Brown was defeated in early May at Silverstone by American Masten Gregory in an Ecurie Ecosse Lister-Jaguar. Two weeks later on the 18th both were at the demanding Spa circuit for the Sports-Car Grand Prix. Scott-Brown was leading Gregory in a close-fought battle when he left the track on a damp patch and suffered burns, in the resulting crash, that proved fatal.

This was a grievous personal and professional loss to Brian Lister and his team. Though inclined to abandon racing, Lister decided that his level of commitment was too great, to his customers and his workforce, to justify withdrawal. Instead he carried on with two works cars driven variously by double Le Mans winner Ivor Bueb, Bruce Halford, Stirling Moss, New Zealander Ross Jensen and visiting fireman Walt Hansgen. Their successes showed that there was life after Archie for the Lister-Jaguar.

Luck was denied the Listers in long-distance racing by the destroked 3.0-liter engines supplied by Jaguar. They let the racers down at Sebring and Le Mans in 1958 and '59. For the latter year Brian decided to go for all-out speed on the Mulsanne straight. "I realized that the Knobbly was not particularly aerodynamic," he related. "But for Le Mans we needed something aerodynamically sound so I engaged Frank Costin." Brian also had in mind an attack on the 200 mph figure with a sports car; he'd considered going for it with the 1957 car but never had the time.

F amed aerodynamicist Frank Costin, frequent partner in Colin Chapman's Lotuses, was lured away from DeHavilland to design a slippery body for the Lister chassis. Costin also designed a new space frame for the Lister, but this wasn't completed while the company was active. The twin-tube chassis for the Costin-bodied cars grew slightly to a 90.8-inch wheelbase with front and rear tracks of 52.0 and 53.5 inches. Brakes as well as wheels were now from Dunlop in the 1959 Lister, unveiled on New Year's Day by Lister, Costin and Ivor "the driver" Bueb.

Again made by Williams & Pritchard, the new

Costin shape was voluminous in search of a lower drag coefficient at the expense of higher frontal area. Wheels were semi-enclosed, a gentle bulge covered the engine and tiny scoops cooled the rear tires. With the Lister reputation now such that what-

Lister at home.

ever emerged from Abbey Road had to be good, the marriage with Costin was seen as magic. The racing contingent snapped up Costin-boded chassis numbers from BHL 121 to 133.

Most of the new cars were kitted out for the Chevy engine while one was adapted to Maserati's 450S V8 for America's John Edgar, who changed his mind and never raced it. In the UK Ivor Bueb and Bruce Halford drove works cars while Peter Blond, Peter Mould, Bill Moss and Mike Anthony were among those who piloted 1959 models. Both Border Reivers for Jim Clark and the Ecurie Ecosse carried on with

earlier-model Listers. One of the latter was a chassis that started life with exposed wheels to compete in that year's 500 Miles of Monza, subsequently rebuilt by Ecurie Ecosse as a sports-racer.

Walt Hansgen and Ed Crawford continued to lead the Stateside Cunningham effort. Walt won the SCCA's Class C Modified honors again with the new car. While Briggs switched to Maseratis for 1960, other campaigners continued to fly the Lister flag. In 1961 an SCCA Modified championship came the way of Pete Harrison's Lister-Chevy.

Looking back, Brian Lister admitted to doubts about his '59 car: "I really regret ever doing the Costin body. If I had my time over again I'd clean up the Knobbly and build lower and smaller like the '57 car and the Lister-Maserati." He got no argument from Stirling Moss, who was candid in his criticism to Brian: "I don't like it as much as your '58 car. I'd much rather drive that. It's smaller and I can see where I'm going." Nor did the vaunted Costin aerodynamics achieve their goal, the cars being no faster on the Mulsanne straight than a D-Type Jaguar.

It's significant that when in 1990, to celebrate the centenary of the family firm, his company laid down a series of new Listers, built by the original craftsmen, Brian Lister chose the Knobbly as the pattern to follow. Four such cars were built and sold through Lawrence Pearce, who with Brian's blessing produced Lister versions of XJS Jaguars from 1986. In 1993 Pearce introduced the Lister Storm, a purpose-built Jaguar-powered sports car, and in 1995 a racing version took to the tracks. Under Pearce's guidance Lister won the FIA's GT Championship in 2000 and is still on the tracks in the 21st Century.

Disappointed with the Costin, money flowing out on the uncompleted space frame, his cars defeated at the British Grand Prix meeting by the new-fangled

Above: The 1959 Lister-Chevy competing in later racing. Wheel houses have been opened out and Halibrand wheels fitted. Listers remain popular in vintage racing.

rear-engined racers, the ever-realistic Brian Lister took stock: "Through the summer of '59 I could see that we weren't going to have very much success. Things were getting very competitive. I hadn't sufficient confidence that we'd be able to keep up the winning streak that we'd enjoyed." Lister decided to suspend his company's competition activity. He announced withdrawal from active participation in racing "for at least a year" on July 23rd, 1959. He promised availability of parts to his existing teams and planned his last works entry for September.

The latter decision went by the boards after the first weekend of August. Brian was with his team at Brands Hatch when Peter Blond crashed badly in practice, luckily without serious injury. Abandoning the entry, Lister was on his way home when he heard on his car radio that courageous Frenchman Jean Behra had died after crashing his Porsche at Berlin's

Avus. Lister had been negotiating through BP to put Behra in a Lister cockpit. Arriving home, his wife José gave him the sad news that Cooper-mounted Ivor Bueb had succumbed from his injuries in a crash at Clermont-Ferrand a week earlier.

"I decided then and there to finish my involvement with motor racing," said Lister. He relapsed only once. Early in 1964 he agreed to use his skills and experience to prepare a brace of Ford-powered Sunbeam Tiger coupes to race at Le Mans. Not under Brian's control, the effort was too hectic, too late and let down in the race by poor engine preparation. Nevertheless, said team chief Marcus Chambers, the cars "looked well turned out" and reached 162 mph on the straight—very nearly as fast as the Costin-Bodied Lister.

"We reckon we built 46 or 48 cars," said Brian Lister with a smile, "of which 60 survive!" There are

probably more than that now with various companies making new versions of the iconic Knobblies. "It's easy enough to do," Lister explained. "They were built on drilling machines, center lathes, universal milling machines—equipment which any reasonable engineering shop will have." And he had no objection: "I take it as a great compliment that people think it's worthwhile to copy the cars."

Worthwhile? What would you be prepared to do to sit in the cockpit of a Lister Knobbly and imagine yourself Walt Hansgen or Archie Scott-Brown, tackling the fast bends of Bridgehampton or Brands Hatch accompanied by the thrust and soaring snarl of a Jaguar six? These are among the vivid memories for which we have to thank Brian Lister and his dedicated team at Abbey Road, home of Cambridge's only automobile company—ever. AQ

The Gilmore Collection

A Pierce-Arrow Dual-Valve Six inadvertently became the catalyst for the Gilmore Car Museum in 1963, when Genevieve Gilmore gave her husband, Donald, the board chairman of the Upjohn pharmaceutical company, a 1920 Pierce-Arrow touring car for his birthday. The Pierce required a thorough restoration, which began outdoors, under a tent, making a project for both Gilmore and his friends. The Pierce sparked a greater interest in cars, leading Gilmore to purchase two nearby farms a mile from his Hickory Corners, Michigan, home. He plotted off 90 acres to create a "playground" for his new hobby. The first two buildings were a restoration shop and a display building. His collection quickly grew to three dozen vehicles. Gilmore and his wife and their friends made the hobby special by dressing in period clothing and driving the cars on Sunday afternoons.

BY BROOKS T. BRIERLEY

As the collection grew, Gilmore began to acquire historic barns and move them to his new farm. One example of this is the Campania, or "C," barn, built in 1897 near the Lake Michigan shoreline, which was used to store spearmint hay for Wrigley's gum.

It was Genevieve Gilmore who suggested the collection be institutionalized as a nonprofit foundation museum. It opened to the public on July 31, 1966. The old barns filled with cars fostered an informal get-close-to-the-cars atmosphere—on the weekends Gilmore and his friends would get together for an afternoon of driving different cars. The Carriage House barn, the first barn the visitor sees when coming in through the front gate, served as the original display area. Donald and Genevieve Gilmore used the attached silo for entertaining, converting it into a sitting area and kitchen.

Today, Michael Spezia, the museum's executive director provides the museum's overview: "The Gilmore Car Museum has been caring for 90 acres of land, 22 buildings and a world-class collection of automobiles and historic collections for nearly forty years. In a comfortable pastoral setting of historic buildings and well-maintained grounds, we strive to offer professional collections and events for the general public, educational community and the automobile enthusiast."

As the museum has grown—there are now eight barns plus a vintage service station, diner and railroad station—that informality has remained. A big paved oval track set among tall pine trees and a vast sloping lawn is the center of outdoor activities. This is the perfect place to both drive and show an automobile or enjoy watching cars pass by or parked during an exhibition.

Special events are still the order of most weekends. The museum officially opens on May 1. The first big events in 2005 represented two different

The Gilmores began acquiring historic barns in which to store the increasing inventory.

aspects of the car hobby. "Miatas & More," a club meet in late May, is about contemporary sports cars. The Classic Car Club Museum's "Grand Experience," held the first weekend of June, includes a concours d'elegance extravaganza. Prior to the concours drive-by, the cars are assembled with in Busby Berkeley-like symmetry around the Museum's oval track.

The museum hosts a wide variety of theme events. One with all-British cars, called "Mad

The Gilmore collection is deep and varied, and its knowledgable onsite mechanics have been an asset from the time the first historic barns were moved to museum grounds.

Dogs and Englishmen British Car Faire," is popular, with rows and rows of parked MGs, Triumphs, Austin Healeys, Sunbeams, et al. The museum's largest weekend turnout is the Kalamazoo Antique Auto Restorers Club "Red Barns Spectacular," when nearly 1,000 cars come out, has become one of the Gilmore's traditions. A twenty-fifth anniversary celebration was held in 2005. This is also the museum's most eclectic event with Brass Era cars sharing the spotlight with modern hot rods and every other era and type of vehicle in between represented.

Extra special are the new weekly "Wednesday Night Cruise-Ins," every Wednesday from 6 to 9 pm, May through October. All vehicles are welcome. About 200 cars of all eras participate. There is no dress code for the cruise-in; the diner is open during the event.

The dispersal of the Gilmore collection into separate structures creates the experience of a country village. That also sharpens the focus of each collection.

Each barn represents a different aspect of the collection. For example, an unusual approach is seen in the barn identified by the letter "G," one of three original museum barns. The museum's special perspective—the depth of its collections—can be experienced in "The Marvin Tamaroff Mascot Collection," in the Barrett Barn together with the Gilmore's own collection of 750-plus mascots and

400 name badges in the "C" Barn. Combined, they make the largest collection of radiator mascots and radiator badges on display in North America. Seeing so many—each well-polished and cared for, and set behind glass cases—reveals a spectacle of shapes and sizes.

The "G" Barn also houses vintage toys and special souvenirs of the Walt Disney movie, "The Gnome-Mobile." Donald Gilmore and Walt Disney were friends; Gilmore supplied the original "Upjohn Pharmacy" for Disneyland's Main Street USA. When Disney began filming "The Gnome-Mobile," Gilmore asked him to sell the 1930 Brewster-bodied Rolls-Royce Sedanca Deville in the movie for his new museum in Hickory Corners. Disney, who had visited the museum, agreed. The movie's shooting

Above: George and Sally's Blue Moon Diner is located at the east side of the property. Left: Located in "G" barn is the movie set of the car featured in Walt Disney's "The Gnome-Mobile."

schedule delayed delivering the car, which Disney used to camouflage a surprise, stating he was "sending a truck with some set pieces you can have." The truck contained the movie set of the car—many times actual size —when the museum acquired the real life version.

Another barn focuses on locally made cars. The nearby city of Kalamazoo was a car-building center for most years of the 20th century. Everyone knows it best for the legendary Checker cabs, yet other interesting marques, including Barley, Hadley-Knight and Roamer, hailed from Kalamazoo, too.

The museum has examples of all of them. There are four Roamers—all representing its 1920s heyday —the largest single group of that marque surviving. The two Barleys there are the only known existing cars.

A bright yellow Shell service station—recreating an early 1930s structure—contrasts with the dark red barns. Its color scheme and architectural design has made it a focal point to stop for a photo—the building and its period gas pumps make a great background for a vintage automobile—or as a highly visible reference point to meet others. Inside is a complete service bay with a number of period artifacts placed inside the office area. Underneath the porte-cochere are hundreds of bricks with names of those who have donated to the museum/station (there

The re-created '30s-era Shell service station is a memorable stop.

Arrow Foundation. Here is a chronological selection of the famous luxury cars with their distinctive fender-mounted headlights. Two coming Pierce-Arrow 100th anniversaries—the inauguration of the new Buffalo factory on Elmwood Avenue in 1907 and the introduction of the Pierce-Arrow truck in 1911—suggest the Foundation is a very busy place behind the scenes.

The collection found in the new "U" Barn, on the east side of the museum, focuses on postwar cars of the 1950s and muscle cars of the 1960s and 1970s. Included are more recent sports cars such as DeLorean and the 1981 Kevlar-bodied BMW M-1 art car.

The Gilmore Museum has become an especially comfortable place to visit with the recent inauguration of "George & Sally's Blue Moon Diner," located at the east side of the property. It is an historic piece, too, originally built in Paterson, NJ., in 1941, becoming "Joe's Diner" in Meriden, Conn. The diner changed hands several times, being "The Blue Moon Diner" when it closed in 1995. It had been empty for several years when the museum purchased it. Nearby residents George and Sally Turner donated the seed money to begin its restoration, creating

are still some unmarked spaces).

The Gilmore Car Museum has grown considerably since 2000. It now has three other museums as partners. The Classic Car Club of America, and the Pierce-Arrow Foundation occupy separate barns. The Tucker Automobile Club of America, in the "C" (or Campania) Barn, includes one of the famous cars. Its archives are highlighted by a recreation of a Tucker sales office, stocked with all the materials needed to place an order.

The recently dedicated Earle Heath Memorial Annex to the Barrett Barn housing the Classic Car Club Museum and Library has a hexagonal shape, topped with a row of clerestory windows. That allows a striking display area for a dozen classic cars. Appropriately, the centerpiece of the opening exhibit

was a 1929 Duesenberg J. Weymann sedan.

One of the museum's secrets is the impressive Noel Thompson library in the "Barrett Barn," which focuses on Classic Era automobiles. The heart of the collection are records of the Derham and Judkins coachbuilder businesses. Here are hundreds of breathtaking original photographs and drawings of some of the greatest automobiles ever built (or planned), plus the business papers describing their history. The wide range of history books filling the nearby shelves helps put everything into perspective.

The museum's original 1920 Pierce-Arrow Model 31 seven-passenger touring car maintains a place of honor in one of the newest barns, at the southern end of the quadrangle, belonging to the Pierce-

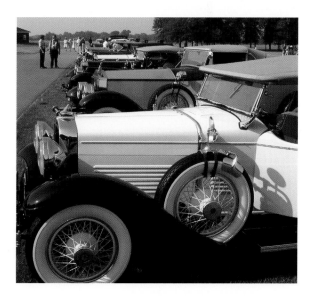

All of the vehicles in the museum are in running condition; many are put into jitney service.

A Special Pungs–Finch at Gilmore

Of all the automobile marques with hyphenated names, none raises more eyebrows and curiosity than the Pungs-Finch. It is one of automotive history's great ironies and surprises. The first hemi engine—the hemispherically—shaped combustion chamber engine design, so closely identified with engines introduced by Chrysler Corporation in the 1950s—was built on Jefferson Avenue in Detroit in 1905 by the Pungs-Finch Auto and Gas Engine Co.

The Gilmore is displaying the only known surviv-

the diner's present name. The Turner's son, Joe, has commented that his late parents' modesty makes it ironic to see their names lit up in neon on the new diner's sign.

The diner, like the museum, is elegant, decorated with wood and fabric, plus the expected chrome fixtures. It offers a great view of the museum grounds in addition to encouraging leisurely lunches or just stopping by to sample some homemade cherry pie a la mode, either inside the diner at a booth or al fresco on the newly created patio/terrace at the far end of the building. Donors names have been engraved into the patio/terrace pavers.

One of the museum's latest features is a jitney service using one of the vintage cars from its collections. The choice of vehicles changes daily—a 1923 Hudson and a 1935 London taxi are two possibilities. All the museum's vehicles are kept in running condition—so the potential choice is quite wide. Going for another ride on the museum grounds is reason alone to make a return visit.

The ultra-rare 1906 Pungs-Finch Limited roadster.

The New York distributor was Charles Duerr, whose C. A. Duerr & Co. represented the more-expensive Royal Tourist. Duerr emphasized the performance aspects of his cars and successfully entered Royals in racing competitions. That also made him a likely proponent of Pungs-Finch's hemi engine. Even so, it was not promoted that way.

Pungs-Finch participated in the Glidden Tours, beginning as Car No. 36 in the 1905 event. William Pungs and his son-in-law, Edward Finch, brought their families to ride with them. We know very little about their run save that they used a touring car. Entering the Pungs-Finch in the Glidden tours was an attempt to build a reliability/durability reputation. However, Pungs-Finch never successfully completed a Glidden Tour. Something was missing in the car's performance—or in the presentation —as there were no accomplishments to publicize. That led C. A. Duerr & Co. to continue to emphasize Royals while Walter Pungs went on building Pungs-Finch cars without his son-in-law. Shortly after models for 1910 were introduced, the business was shut down. **AQ**

ing Pungs-Finch, a 1906 Limited roadster, courtesy of the museum's chair, Bill Parfet. The car was in a Detroit warehouse in the 1950s when collector Henry Austin Clark found it. He had the car restored for his Long Island Museum. Later, the roadster belonged to the Pate Museum in Texas and then with a private individual in California. It was readied for the 2006 Pebble Beach Concours d'Elegance.

Pungs-Finch was introduced in 1905 as a mid-priced car with a four-cylinder engine. This model was technically interesting with shaft drive and sliding gear transmission. In 1906, a more upmarket model was added, called the Limited. Prices for these cars began at $3,000. Here was a special 60hp 528cid (about 10 liters) four-cylinder motor—with a 5 3/4-inch bore and 6 1/2-inch stroke—set on a 111-inch wheelbase chassis.

Outside, the Limited roadster looks no different than any of its two-seater contemporaries. Riding in it today can still unleash its unique mechanical traits. Both driver and passenger sit completely exposed to the elements and the engine's hearty sound.

There were never many Pungs-Finch—perhaps several hundred were built during five years of production. A modest network of dealers in New York, Philadelphia and Chicago sold them.

What stopped such an intriguing product with shaft drive and the first hemi engine? By mid-1906, Edward Finch had taken a second job as manager of the technical department at Packard. Reports of differences between Pungs and Finch are said to have led to a complete break. Even so, in July 1907, the Pungs and Finch families made their last Glidden Tour together - which may have completed their estrangement.

Another negative force appears to have come from the dealer network.

THE LAST CORD
Death in Beauty

The dynasty of Errett Lobban Cord is memorialized by some of the world's most magnificent machines. The sexy Auburns of the late '20s. The incredible Duesenberg J. Marking the end of the dynasty was the Cord—namely the 810 and 812, models emblematic of the company's rush to save itself from demise during a period that combined some of the industry's most extraordinary talent. In Cord's swan song we see death in the beauty of monumental design.

EXCERPTED FROM "ERRETT LOBBAN CORD" BY GRIFFITH BORGESON

As Gordon Buehrig told the story over the years, when things began to get tight at Duesenberg, he moved on to General Motors Styling, where he began working on Feb. 28, 1933. During the spring he designed a car around the idea of keeping its engine clean. He said in Rolling Sculpture: "The scheme was to have two radiators located between the hood and front fenders and to block off direct air flow to the engine. It was a very good idea but it set up a package problem that was bound to give a new look to the front end."

On Sept. 20, Buehrig received a call from Duesenberg president Harold Ames, who said that he had an idea he would like to discuss, inviting him to come to Indianapolis during the coming weekend for that purpose. The meeting took place and Buehrig learned about Ames's idea for a much less expensive Duesenberg, to consist of "a trick body design" on an Auburn straight-eight chassis. Buehrig agreed to leave

1937 Cord 812 SC, a most desirable phaeton.

GM and return to Duesenberg, to do the design work on this intriguing project. The idea of a "hermetically sealed engine compartment" of course was not practical for various reasons, but Ames did like the novelty of the approach. On Nov. 7, Buehrig showed him a pair

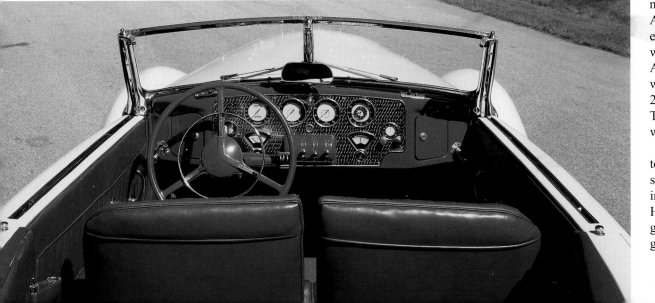

of sketches, he liked them, and the project was off and running. Buehrig worked out 1/8-scale drawings, then made a model to that scale. Ames approved it, full-scale drawings were made and passed to Phil Derham, who had the body built by Weymann in Indianapolis. While this was going on, August "Augie" Duesenberg, now with the company, worked on the modified Auburn chassis and the problem of the unorthodox external radiators. They proved to be inadequate in hot weather. The body was finished and mounted on the Auburn chassis in February of '34, but a big shakeup was underway in Auburn at the same time, and on Feb. 27, Ames, Buehrig and Augie were transferred there. The Baby Duesenberg project was shelved and the car was left in storage in Indianapolis.

Ames recalled this period a bit differently. According to him, it was Buehrig who called him in late 1933, to say that he had a new design for an automobile. It involved the idea of keeping the engine clean and Harley Earl had turned it down, saying, "People don't give a damn if the engine is dirty or not. The idea is no good." Buehrig still thought that it had merit and wanted to show it to Ames. At that period, Ames worked in Auburn during the week and flew to Indianapolis weekends to keep tabs on the little that was happening at Duesenberg. Ames recalled:

"I met him in Indianapolis on a Sunday, and he had this sketch. It had radiators between the hood and the fender on either side. The front end had nothing on it—it was just round, plain. I said, 'Gee, that's interesting. We could even put Roosevelt's picture on the front end.' I remember that detail well. I told him that if he wanted to come back I'd build one, which we did, with the radiators there. We tried every way under the sun to develop rigidity between the fender and the hood, but you'd drive it a couple of hundred miles and you'd have a cracked radiator. We tried and tried, and it wouldn't work. So, we put the radiator aside, and wrapped the louvers around the hood. Prior to that, car hoods always had been lifted from the side. This one had to

be lifted from the front and was hinged at the back. That's how that design came into being."

In Auburn, Ames and Buehrig became totally involved in the 851 facelift and Augie in supercharging the car's engine. Such an engine in a '34 Auburn was shipped to E.L. Cord in England that summer. Buehrig noted in his diary that it was on June 24 that he and Denny Duesenberg, Fred's son, drove the Baby Dues from Indianapolis to Auburn, which must have been a stunning treat for witnesses along the way. It had been decided to resume the project, but it is unclear whether it was already decided to use that general body design for a new Cord, dropping the small Duesenberg, or if that decision came slightly later. Apparently the front-wheel-drive (fwd) chassis already had been designed and built in scale-model mockup form, because work began without delay on the design and engineering of a body to fit it. Considerable change was required

Top: The enterprising Errett Lobban Cord. Above: This photo of chief designer Gordon Buehrig was taken in 1966. Right: 1937 Cord 812 with rare side mount.

because the car would be a fwd and would be powered by a new V8 engine. Moreover, it was the decision of chief body engineer Roy Anderson and his immediate aides to use all-steel monocoque construction. A ¼-scale clay model was completed in late summer 1934. As in the case of the Baby Dues, the body department developed the full-scale body drafts from the scale model; a full-size mockup of the fwd body never was

Right: Harold Ame's patent drawings for the Cord headlights. Herbert Snow's contribution, opposite page. Below: August Duesenberg's sketch of his cooling system invention for Cord.

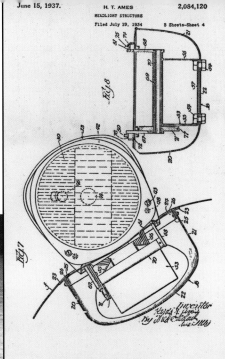

built. The job progressed rapidly and by the end of December the die models were nearing completion. Then, at the turn of the year and for reasons known only to top management, the project was dropped. What happened would seem to be perfectly obvious. With the end of fiscal 1934, the company's cash surplus consisted of a record deficit of almost $4 million and its stock never had been worth so little. Looking at its balance sheet, nobody in his right mind would give a nickel's credit to this expert loser.

Charles Errett ("Charlie") Cord, E.L.'s son, had a vivid recollection of when his father first saw Buehrig's coffin-nose design. The family was installed in the country place in England and it was well before E.L. took the boys back to

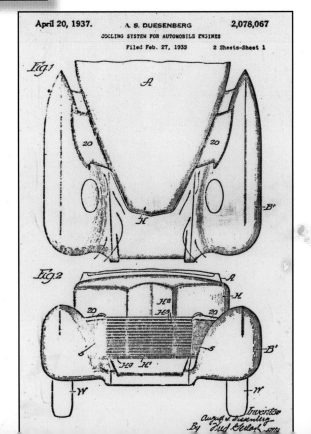

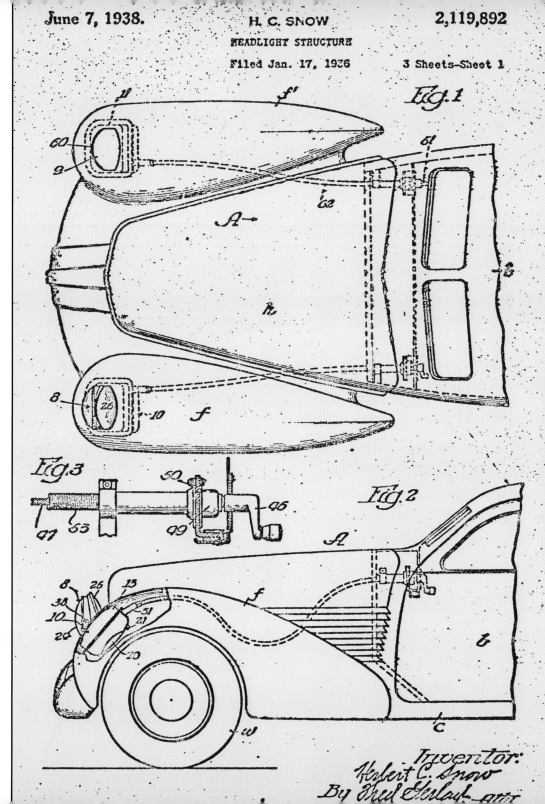

Fig.1

Fig.3

Fig.2

Inventor:
Herbert C. Snow
By Fred Gerlach attr

school in the fall. Thus it was in the summer of 1934 that three or four photos of a complete car, taken against the back entrance of the Duesenberg factory, arrived in the mail, probably from Ames. These photos had to be of the Weymann-built Baby Dues. Thus, E.L. had absolutely nothing to do with the body concept, perhaps for the first time since he had taken over at Auburn. This is of particular interest in view of the fact that, if he had a favorite among the cars that his companies built, it was the 810/12 Cord. This circumstance also illustrates the extent to which Ames's thinking paralleled E.L.'s and how far Ames could go before checking with the boss.

Buehrig filed for a design patent (Des. 93,451, assigned to Cord Corp.) on the Baby Dues on May 17, 1934. The patent drawings are copied faithfully from the above-mentioned photos of the newly completed car. Clearly visible were the headlights that swung open from the inner sides of the front fenders, and the trick radiators. Without noting Ames's involvement, Buehrig said in his book, speaking of the disappearing headlights: "Ames was particularly proud of this innovation because it was an idea taken from the landing lights of the Stinson airplane. Stinson Aircraft was then a part of the Cord Corporation."

Ames was the one who made the disappearing headlight idea work. The Auburn Cord Duesenberg Museum archives contain a very ample collection of Auburn and Cord patents, including Ames's No. 2,084,120, filed on June 15, 1934, and also assigned to Cord Corp. It is extensively detailed, consisting of 1,043 lines of fine-print specification and a dozen drawings. Among other things, it confirms in no uncertain way Ames's activity as a mechanical designer in his own right. The Ames system was used on the prototype Cord 810 as well as on the Baby Dues. For production, however, another system was adopted, which Buehrig says was better, in which, of course, the lights are pivoted in the leading surfaces of the front fenders. The individual who devised this system and filed for a patent on it on Jan. 17, 1936, was Herb Snow. Snow's patent was assigned to the Auburn Automobile Co.

As for the trick radiators, Augie did a very proper job of engineering the entire cooling system that permitted the principle to work. Although the external radiator idea had been abandoned even before the Baby Dues project was dropped, Augie obviously saw enough promise in it to take the trouble to apply for a patent on his solution at the late date of Feb. 27, 1935. It is numbered 2,078,067 and was assigned to Cord Corp.

Buehrig filed for a design patent on what would be the 810 body on Aug. 5, 1935, receiving number Des. 97,697. It was assigned to the Auburn Automobile Co. It still showed the Ames-type headlights but now had the "Venetian blind" louvers of the definitive type, as well as the seminal three lights in the rear deck lid and small locking door for access to the fuel-tank filler cap. Gone were the fender struts, the external radiators, and now both doors were hinged on a common

central pillar, instead of both being hinged at the back. The rear quarter-windows had been deleted, but the same Cagin Speedster-type sliver of a rear window persisted. Buehrig filed for yet another design patent on May 11, 1936, receiving number Des. 99,973. It covered merely the appearance of the hood, indicating a hump in the bottom louver, over the hump in the front apron, and a slight ridge down the center of the top of the hood. It, too, was assigned to the Auburn Automobile Co.

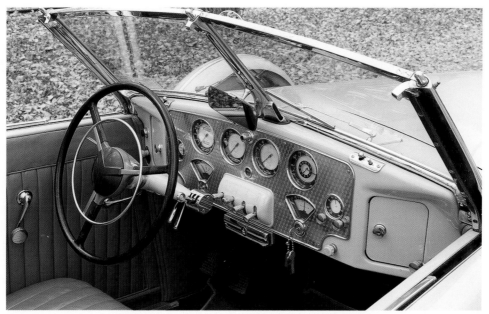

Hi-tech instrumentation—for the day—appeared in latter-day Cord models, lending a sense of sport to the interior.

While a very great deal of thoroughly deserved print has been devoted to the coachwork of the last Cords, the recognition given to their mechanical side has been unjustly slight. To begin with, their V8 Lycoming engine has been underestimated and widely ignored. Its block and crankcase were a single cast-iron unit, and thus commendably rigid. Such construction had been pioneered by the Ford V8, at a cost that was

astronomical, but which could be amortized over millions of units sold. One has to wonder if there ever was any more prospect of amortizing the Lycoming V8 than there had been for the engine of the Model J.

With bore and stroke of 3.5 x 3.75 inches, it had a super-short and very avant-garde stroke/bore ration of merely 1.07 to one. Its displacement of 289 cu. in. was modest for a car of its intended class, but it delivered an ample 125 bhp at 3500 rpm, and did so at very low piston speed. The engine valve arrangement was described erroneously as being L-head, a conclusion suggested by its external appearance. Instead, it was original and exotic, consisting of almost horizontal valves and a single very high camshaft, giving an almost overhead-camshaft effect. The combustion chambers were compact and wedge-shaped. Domed pistons helped to produce a compression ratio of 6.5 to one, a bit high for the time. The engine would have been perfectly at home among the Detroit V8s of the '50s. Its specific power output probably was the highest among American cars in 1936, with the exception of the twin-cam J Dues.

By odd coincidence, the 810's unusual top-end arrangement was very similar to that of van Ranst's Packard V12. To find anything like them, one had to go back to a V12 that Harry Miller had designed and built in 1917.

Ahead of the 810's flywheel came the clutch and a short drive shaft, which also was the main shaft of the change-speed transmission. This longitudinally oriented gearbox was located ahead of the final-drive gears and had four forward speeds, a real rarity in American practice. Top gear was an overdrive and all but bottom gear were synchronized. Good Rzeppa constant-velocity outer U-joints were used this time. According to published drawings, the 810 front-end geometry provided for a small amount of negative steering offset, meaning that the king-pin axis touched the pavement outboard of the center of the tire contact patch. This widely imitated breakthrough has been credited to the designers of the fwd Oldsmobile Toronado, no one remembering that the harried designers of the 810 had put this important principle to work 30 years

system a preselector capacity and an inherently slow operating rate.

While the 810's rear suspension was purely traditional, by semi-elliptic springs, its front suspension was one of the pioneer independent types to be adopted in the United States. It was unique in utilizing box-section

Kublin, aided by L.H. "Slim" Davidson. Again, nameless others must have made their contributions.

Buehrig has told how, early one Sunday morning at the beginning of July 1935, Faulkner called him at home, saying that there would be a meeting of the Cord Corp. board in Chicago the following morning. A body

Style and power earmarks the last Cords. Streamlined cues coupled with supercharged engines set the 810s and 812s apart. The European-style turn indicator (below left) came on this export model.

before. They were the fwd specialists, after all, and had been stockpiling ideas for improvements since the heyday of the L-29.

The 810's transaxle unit was a clever and elegant piece of engineering. Its author remains nameless, although we know that it was built for Cord by the Detroit Gear Co. The problem of shifting gears was solved by means of a new Bendix product, called the Electric Hand, which used solenoid switches and inlet-manifold vacuum to make the changes, taking its orders from a small manual switch on the steering column. This did away with all the problems of establishing a mechanical liaison between the passenger compartment and the distant gearbox. It had the disadvantage of being a bit sluggish in its functioning. The engine could be started only when the tiny shift lever was in neutral position, after which the lever could be moved in its diminutive gate to the next desired gear. The change of gears would not take place, however, until the clutch pedal was fully depressed and the foot lifted momentarily from the throttle. This gave the

trailing arms and a single transverse leaf spring at the front. Delco lever-type double-acting shock absorbers were employed all around.

We probably never will know to whom credit is due for the many excellent features of this quite outstanding chassis. At least a good part of the credit for the engine goes to Forest S. "Bill" Baster, then chief engineer at Lycoming. The whole program, of course, was guided by Herb Snow. Under him was chief engineer George

for the fwd car planned for the '36 model year had to be chosen then. Herb Snow wanted to use the existing Auburn body, while Faulkner favored the Buehrig design. Could Gordon get his hands on some good photos of the clay model of the coffin-nose car? The photos, which did not yet exist, were there in Chicago when the meeting began some 24 hours later. The verdict was, "Build it!"

Charlie Cord's firsthand memories of the genesis of the 810 differ markedly from Buehrig's. He cannot agree that only a small clay model existed in early July 1935. He got out of school and flew to Auburn well before that time. There they had their first impressive encounter with a real, full-scale, in-the-metal 810. It was in the experimental engineering department, at the rear of the Administrative Building. They did not witness the car in operation, but Charlie feels certain that it was a running machine at that time. Concerning the approval of the board, there was just one man who did the approving. Charlie is emphatically sure that his father had approved the 810 body design "long before the morning of July 7, 1935."

The 810's tooling and construction of a pilot run gave Auburn a short-term lease on life that would tide it over until, the SEC willing, it could float its $2.8 million debenture issue. It was hoped that that would keep it going until deliveries and cash flow could begin.

An awful complication was that the American Manufacturers' Association, which had taken over the big-time auto-show circuit, had moved the opening of the show season up to Nov. 2. Another was that, in order to qualify as an exhibitor, one supposedly had to have produced at least 100 units of the new model-year line. There were 116 days in which to pull off this impossibility. There simply was not time in which to get the production line in to operation. The needed cars would have to be built by hand.

Some of the published sources say that the 100 cars somehow got built in time for the opening of the show season, in New York. Others put the total at 11. All seem to agree that none of them had transmissions, making it irrelevant whether they had engines or not. They say that the convertibles were shown with their disappearing tops in the down position, since they had no tops at all. They say that the cars were tied down

This 1937 Cord 812 SC Sportsman convertible was a right-hand drive export. Inset: Another 1937 812 SC.

THE 1937 CORD MODEL 812 Supercharged Convertible Phaeton Sedan.

against their springs to compensate for their lack of mechanical ballast.

This data was also contradicted by Charlie Cord. Sometime during July 1935, what appeared to be the same early 810 that he had seen in Auburn arrived at the big house in Beverly Hills. It appeared to have been driven there by a team of three or four factory men, who did considerable work on the car in the big garage there. Charlie recalled that by Sept. 1, when he began working as a car salesman, the car and its crew had left.

He recalled that a second fully operational 810 arrived there no later than early October. At about the time of the Los Angeles Auto Show in November '35, in which Charlie worked as a salesman, a second operational 810 arrived at the big house. It probably came on the same train that brought the cars for the show. Charlie remembered vividly demonstrating the car to a number of friends. Finally, he was positive that a cabriolet was on display at the Los Angeles Show, with its top up.

In any case, the cars were divine. They were and remain one of the triumphs of industrial design in the 20th century. Had immediate delivery been possible, or had introduction been deferred until delivery was possible, the course of history would have been quite different, with the 810 perhaps reaping the full harvest of the success that it so richly deserved. Only frustration was possible, given a few hand-built cars.

It was not until Aug. 10, 1935, that work began at Connersville, Ind., on setting up the assembly line. That was just 84 days before the eager customers would start flocking to the shows, checkbooks in hand. It would be another 74 days beyond that before, on Jan. 15, 1936, the first 810 body would leave the master welding fixture on the Connersville assembly line. It took another 30 days to get the paint and trim departments and the line itself fully operational. Only then could deliveries be thought of. It was then that service managers from more than 100 dealerships all over the country were given a quick technical introduction to the new fwd car and its esoteric maintenance procedures. According to the Connersville News Examiner for Feb. 15, Roy Faulkner

told the assembled specialists, to whom would fall the responsibility of dealing with eventual mechanical problems:

"We realize that anything that is new and different is in the spotlight, and as a result we have spent many extra thousands of dollars and many weeks of time in making this new Cord as near faultless as a mechanical unit can be built. We have tested beyond anything, to my knowledge, that has ever been done in the automotive industry."

If you care to listen.

According to Ames, there were no test cars until well after show time. It was the lucky customers who got to do most of the road research. Their findings, in the form of complaints, were routed through the company's specially established "free technical consulting service," which passed them on to the departments concerned for the taking of appropriate action. What was genuinely amazing was how wonderfully well this force of highly motivated men—not known for their high salaries—had done its job in the first place.

They seemed to thrive on adversity, rising magnificently to meet every handicap, in terms of dramatically limited time, money, research and development. Their espirit de corps had to be phenomenal.

They pulled it off like champions. Very quickly, the car was quite acceptably debugged and became a marked critical success. But it had been aborted into the world, rather than enjoying a proper birth, and that handicap no one could overcome. The gravest of all the consequences of this misfortune was that deliveries did not begin until the month of March 1936. In the almost six months that had elapsed since the 810's electrifying presentation, its competitors, and others with private axes to grind, could flood the world at their leisure with rumors that were highly destructive to the 810. Result: this super-mousetrap, this marvel, priced from $1,995, found buyers to justify the building of only 1,174 units during 1936. The following year, that of the Cord 812, prices were raised by $450 and supercharged models were available for another $415. By the time the curtain came down, in August 1937, only 1,149 of these had been built.

The handling and roadability of these cars were outstanding, in the opinions of some very severe judges. Their performance was terrific. The small, slippery body helped to give the unblown cars a top speed of about 95 mph. With their 2.75-to-one overdrive top gear they would cruise all day at 80 mph without effort and barely a whisper of noise. They would accelerate from zero to 60 in about 20 seconds, in spite of the slow action of the electrical gear-changing device. Their fuel consumption was by far the best in their performance class.

The first few blown 812s developed about 175 bhp at 4200 rpm, but this soon was increased to about 190 bhp, equal to a most impressive .66 bhp/cu. in. The sturdy engine supported this high output very well. Zero to 60 times dropped to just under 14 seconds, with a fuel-consumption penalty that was less than one might expect. Ab Jenkins drove an 812S to a series of new American stock-car records on the Bonneville Salt Flats; while averaging 101.72 mph for 24 hours, he got about 10 miles to the gallon of fuel. His best speed was 108.34 mph for 10 miles. Because he was running for stock-car records, Jenkins was obliged by the AAA to use original equipment road tires. Others, which would have allowed the maintenance of higher speeds, without shredding treads, were readily available.

Cash-flow-wise, Auburn never got near the break-even point in its last automotive fling. If it could have shown a theoretical profit of $500 on each of the 2,323 cars it built, that would have amounted to just $1,161,500—merely a fraction of its investment in the exercise. Beyond that, there was Lycoming's costly investment in the V8 engine, from which it got no further mileage. But, product-wise, the last Cord was a masterpiece. It is summed up ideally in one of the tributes that Buehrig preserved:

"For sheer taste, for functional correctness and for beauty the 810 Cord is the best design the American industry has ever produced."

As noted, it seems to have been E.L.'s favorite. In his last years he was known to say, with a hint of grudging pride and satisfaction, "It still looks pretty good, doesn't it." It was a statement, not a question.

NOTES AND N&C COMMENTARY

CONTACTING AQ

Automobile Quarterly, ISSN 0005-1438, ISBN 978-1-59613-051-7, is published quarterly by Automobile Heritage Publishing and Communications, LLC. Editorial and publication offices: 800 East 8th Street, New Albany, Indiana, USA 47150. Telephone (812) 948-AUTO (2886); fax (812) 948-2816; e-mail info@autoquarterly.com; Web site www.autoquarterly.com.

SUBSCRIPTION SERVICE

For subscriptions, back issues, indexes, reader service, changes of address, and order entry, call (866) 838-2886. If calling from Indiana or outside the U.S., call (812) 948-2886. Back issue prices start at $25.95, plus shipping. For domestic subscription orders: 1 year (4 issues), $79.95; 2 years (8 issues), $149.95; 3 years (12 issues), $199.95. for Canadian orders: 1 year, $99.95; 2 years, $189.95; 3 years, $259.95. For all other international orders: 1 year, $109.95; 2 years, $209.95; 3 years, $289.95. Mastercard, Visa, or American Express are accepted. Order online at www.autoquarterly.com. To order by mail, please send check or money order to *AQ/Automobile Quarterly*, 1950 Classic Car Circle, P.O. Box 1950, New Albany, IN 47151. The fax number for orders is (812) 948-2816.

POSTMASTER

Please send all changes of address to: *Automobile Quarterly*, P.O. Box 1950, New Albany, IN 47151. Periodical postage paid at New Albany, Indiana, and at additional mailing offices.

LEGAL NOTICE

Entire contents copyright 2005 by Automobile Heritage Publishing and Communications, LLC. Library of Congress Catalog Number 62-4005. *AQ, Automobile Quarterly*, Quatrafoil, and are registered trademarks of Automobile Heritage Publishing and Communications, LLC. All rights reserved. Reproduction in whole or in part without permission is prohibited.

OPPORTUNITY

Details of fund raising programs for car clubs and automobile museums are available by calling: (812) 948-AUTO (2886).

Cover & Contents

Art by John Francis Marsh.

Frontispiece

Coker has also developed an annual award, the Coker Golden Tire Award, which will honor two people who actively drive and show their collector cars and urge others to do the same. Contestants can start showing their efforts to further the hobby by submitting photos and documentation to the Coker Web site (www.coker.com).

Color photography from AQ Photo and Research Archives.

Alfa Romeo Monza

Special thanks to the car's owner, William Binnie, for opening up his garage and allowing us a peek at his amazing Alfa.

Black-and-white photography: p. 6 (top) from the Benciolini Collection; p. 6 (bottom) from the Geoff Goddard Collection; pp. 7 (top), 8 (top) courtesy of the author; p. 7 (bottom) from Alfa Romeo Archives.

Color photography: pp. 4, 9-17 by Philip Scalia; p. 8 courtesy of William Binnie.

Motoring Through Tough Times

With great thanks to *Automobile Quarterly* for sponsoring this four-part series that we have loosely called "Motoring Through Tough Times," I hope the reader has enjoyed these looks at the some of the 20th century automobile's most defining moments in World War I, the Great Depression, World War II, and the 1970s. These are not times that produced great cars. Indeed the great cars that came out of them were in defiance of their days, not demonstrative of them. Nonetheless, I hope the reader will come away from these essays with the overall idea that what happens in history didn't have to happen, that choices were made, that ideas, good and bad, played out, and that public policy indeed matters, especially with cars. The automobile is truly the most indomitable feature of the modern era. No conflict, no economics, and no politics could destroy the people's love for cars. Automobiles have been down and out by circumstance or design, but never from the people's hearts, their heavy right feet, and that ever-willing check book. I wish also to thank my parents and my children for suffering through and lovingly supporting this project, my students for enjoying the stories and, hopefully, learning along the way (kids love cars!), and the Ladd family for keeping the lights on while I vainly tried to finish on time.

Black-and-white photography: pp. 18, 20, 21, 22 from the National Archives; p. 26 courtesy of Ford Motor Co. and Wieck Media Services.

Color photography: pp. 23, 25, 27 courtesy of Ford Motor Co. and Wieck Media Services; p. 24 courtesy of GM Media Archives.

Bibliography

Crandall, Robert W., et. al, *Regulating the Automobile*, Brookings Institution, Washington, DC, 1986;
Kemper, James S., Jr, "The Highway Safety Legislation: Its Implications for Insurance," *Journal of Risk and Insurance*, Vol. 35, No. 1, March 1968, pp. 67-73;
Marxsen, Craig S. "Relative Prices: Automobiles Were Driven By Regulation," Web published, University of Nebraska at Kearney, accessed at http://www.westga.edu/~bquest/2004/prices.htm#change, June, 2006;
Mueller, Marti, "Nader: From Auto Safety to Permanent Crusade," *Science*, Vol 166, No. 3908, Nov. 21, 1969, pp. 979-983;
New York Times, New York Times Co., 1955-1983;
Wall Street Journal, Dow Jones & Co., 1965-1983;
White, Lawrence, W., "The American Automobile Industry and the Small Car, 1945-1970," *Journal of Industrial Economics*, Vol. 20, No. 2, April 1972, pp 179-192;
Wright, J. Patrick, *On a Clear Day You Can See General Motors: John Z. DeLorean's Look Inside the Automotive Giant*, Wright Enterprises, Grosse Pointe, Michigan, 1979;
Yates, Brock, *The Decline and Fall of the American Automobile Industry*, Empire Books, New York, 1983.

Appreciating Apperson

Special appreciation goes to the following people and institutions: Kay Frazer at the Elwood Haynes Museum; Kelli Austin, executive director of the City of Firsts Automotive Heritage Museum; James Gardenhire at Northern Indiana Supply Co.; Dave Griffey; and Gale Leiter at the Howard County Historical Museum.

Black-and-white photography: pp. 30 (right), 31, 35 (right), 37, 40 (background) from the AQ Photo and Research Archives; p. 30 (bottom), 44 from the Elwood Haynes Museum; pp. 33, 34, 35 (top and bottom left), 41 from the Howard County Historical Museum; p. 38 courtesy of Indianapolis Motor Speedway; pp. 39, 40 (inset) from the Auburn Cord Duesenberg Museum

Color photography: pp. 28, 29, 32, 43, 45 by Kelly Bergman; pp. 31, 42 by Tracy Powell; p. 36 from the Elwood Haynes Museum; pp. 37, 38, 39, 41, 44 from the AQ Photo and Research Archives.

Bibliography

Falck, J.D., interview notes, 2002;
Griffey, Dave. *Beyond the Pioneer: The Impact of "America's First Mechanically Successful Automobile"*. Trafford, Victoria, B.C., Canada, 2006;
Horvath, Dennis. *Cruise IN: A Guide to Indiana's Automotive Past and Present*. Publishing Resources, Indianapolis, 1997.

GM Design Chiefs

For sharing their stories, the author thanks Chuck Jordan, Wayne Cherry and Ed Welburn. Thanks also to John Kyros at GM Media Archive.

Black-and-white photography: pp. 48, 58 from the AQ Photo and Research Archives; pp. 50, 51, 56, 57, 59 courtesy of GM Photo Archive.

Color photography: pp. 46-47 rendering by Dan Bulleit; pp. 49, 50, 53, 54, 56, 58 (right), 59 (bottom) from the AQ Photo and Research Archives; pp. 52, 55, 58 (left), 59 (top), 60-63 courtesy of GM Media Archive.

Bibliography

"Architecture for the Future: GM Constructs a 'Versailles of Industry'", *LIFE Magazine*, May 1956;
Barach, John. "Cadillac History", motorera.com, 2005;
Baulch, Vivian M. "Harley Earl, Father of the 'Dream Car'", The Detroit News, cars.com, 2005;
Bell, James D. "LaSalle, Companion Car to Cadillac", *Automobile Quarterly*, Vol. 5 No. 3, 1967;
Bruce-Briggs, B. "Designs for Driving from General Motors",

(continued on page 118)

THE 12th ANNUAL
Amelia Island
Concours d'Elegance
March 9-11, 2007   The Ritz-Carlton, Amelia Island, Florida
The Golf Club of Amelia Island at Summer Beach

2007 AMELIA >

HONORING
Derek Bell MBE

FEATURING
Cars of the
Great Road Races
and their
Legendary Drivers

Sir Stirling Moss
John Surtees MBE
John Fitch
Hershel McGriff
Brian Redman
Vic Elford

1953 Porsche 550 Coupé
The Collier Collection

1953 Ferrari 340/375
Jon Shirley

www.ameliaconcours.org

GM Design Chiefs (Bibliography continued from page 116)

Wall Street Journal, March 16, 1984;

Burton, Jerry. *Zora Arkus-Duntov: The Legend Behind Corvette,* Bentley Publishers, 2002

Cherry, Wayne. Interview, Amelia Island, Florida, 2006;

Crippen, David. "The Reminiscences of William L. Mitchell", Automotive Design Oral Histories, Benson Ford Research Center, The Henry Ford Museum, 1985;

Earl, Richard. Earl Family Archives, carofthecentury.com/earl family archives, 2005;

Einstein, Paul A. "GM's Wayne Cherry, The Chief of Style at GM Talks About Design Leadership", thecarconnection.com, 1999;

"Harley Earl Recalls LaSalle", *Automobile Quarterly*, Vol. 5 No. 3, 1967;

"Harley Earl's Greatest Hits", Automobile Photo Gallery, automobile.com, 2005;

"Harley J. Earl", Industrial Designers Society of America, idsa.com, 2005;

Jordan, Chuck. Interview, 2006;

Lamm, Michael. "Harley Earl's California Years", *Automobile Quarterly*, Vol. 20 No. 1, 1982;

Lamm, Michael and Holls, David. *A Century of American Car Design*, Lamm-Morada Publishing, 1996-97;

McMinn, Strother, "A Shark is Not a Grouper", *Automobile Quarterly*, Vol. 26 No. 2, 1988;

Marcus, Frank. "The Corvettes that Never Were", *Motor Trend Classic*, Issue Two, 2005;

Patton, Phil. "The Cars GM Didn't Want You to See", forbes.com, 2001;

Rothenberg, Randall. "Works of the Modern Master: Harley Earl, Profiling the Man who Changed America Forever", *AdAge*, 2002;

Scharchburg, Richard. "Automotive Hollywood, The Battle for Body Beautiful", *Collection of Industrial History*, Kettering University, 1999;

Speilvogel, Carl. "Along the Highways and Byways of Finance", *New York Times*, March 25, 1956;

Welburn, Edward T. Jr. Interview, New York, 2006;

Winding-Sorensen, Jon. "75 Years of General Motors Design", Car Design News, cardesignnews.com, 2003;

Zazarine, Paul, "The Life and Times of Harley Earl", *Collectible Automobile*, December 2005/February 2006.

Art Gallery with John Francis Marsh

Special thanks to this issue's magnificent artist.
Color photography courtesy of John Francis Marsh.

Lister Racers

The author is grateful to Brian Lister and his wife José for hospitality extended to him in the course of researching the remarkable story of Lister cars. He sends his thanks also to Suffolk's 1066 Classic Car Club, at whose meeting the author first met Brian Lister, prompting the idea for this story. Mr. Lister has reviewed the text of the article, but any errors of omission or commission are the author's. Brian Lister kindly made available a number of images from his personal archive which appear in this article Research for the article was conducted in the Ludvigsen Library, which holds numerous cuttings and articles about Lister cars from contemporary periodicals. Both Doug Nye and Michael Bowler kindly provided the author with printouts of their personal records concerning the provenance and ownership of the various Lister cars. The newest edition of Nye's *Powered by Jaguar* contains his updated records on these cars.

All photography courtesy of the Ludvigsen Library.

Bibliography

Edwards, Robert. *Archie and the Listers,* Patrick Stephens, Sparkford, 1995;

Nye, Doug. *Powered by Jaguar,* Motor Racing Publications, London, 1980;

Gauld, Graham. *Ecurie Ecosse,* Graham Gauld Public Relations, Edinburgh, 1992.

The Gilmore Collection

The author would like to thank Michael Spezia, Executive Director of the Gilmore Car Museum and Jay Follis, Director of Marketing, for their help assembling information on the museum. Thanks also to Kim Miller of the AACA Library and Research Center, the staff of the Library of Congress and Mark Patrick and Barbara Thompson of the National Automotive History Collection for helping reveal the Pungs-Finch's obscure history.

Black-and-white photography courtesy of the Gilmore Car Museum.

Color photography: pp. 90-94, 96 (top) courtesy of the Gilmore Car Museum; pp. 95, 96 (bottom), 97 (bottom) by Don Getz; p. 97 (top) from the AQ Photo and Research Archives.

Bibliography

"Automobile Notes of Interest." *New York Times*, July 7, 1907;

"Big Entry List For Motor Tour." *New York Times*, July 7, 1907;

"Pungs-Finch." *Cycle and Automobile Trade Journal*, March 1906;

"Pungs-Finch Indeed." *Automobile Quarterly*, Vol. 8, No. 1;

Pungs-Finch Touring Car ad, *MoToR*, January 1905;

The Book of Detroiters, A. N. Marquis & Company, 1908 (transcribed by www.usgennet.org);

"The Pungs-Finch 1905 Four-Cylinder Touring Car." *Cycle and Automobile Trade Journal*, October 1904.

Contact Information

Gilmore Car Museum
6865 Hickory Road
Hickory Corners, MI 49060
Phone: 269-671-5089
Web site: www.gilmorecarmuseum.org

The Last Cord

Excerpted from *Errett Lobban Cord* by Griffith Borgeson, published by Automobile Quarterly.

All photography from the AQ Photo and Research Archives.

Coda

Color photography courtesy of Volkswagen of America, Inc.

Back Cover

Debossment of Apperson mark.

STATEMENT OF OWNERSHIP INFORMATION, MANAGEMENT AND CIRCULATION REQUIRED BY 39 U.S.C. 3685

Date of filing, September 2006. AQ/Automobile Quarterly is published four times a year at P.O. Box 1950, New Albany, IN 47151. Subscription price $79.95. Full name and complete mailing address of publishing director is Gerald L. Durnell, 800 E. 8th Street, New Albany, IN 47150. The owner is Automobile Heritage Publishing and Communications, LLC: Gerald L. Durnell, Managing Partner: P.O. Box 1950, New Albany, IN 47151. Names and addresses of holders of record of 1 percent or more of Automobile Heritage Publishing and Communications, LLC are Gerald L. Durnell, P.O. Box 1950, New Albany, IN 47151; L. Kaye Bowles-Durnell, P.O. Box 1950, New Albany, IN 47151. There are no bond holders, mortgages, or security holders. A. Total number of copies printed (net press run). Average number of copies printed each issue during preceding 12 months: 9,063. Actual number of copies of single issue published nearest to filing date: 10,450. B. Paid circulation. 1. Sales through dealers and carriers, street vendors, and counter sales. Average number of copies each issue during preceding 12 months: 0. Actual number of copies of single issue published nearest to filing date: 0. 2. Mail subscriptions. Average number of copies each issue during preceding 12 months: 7,375. Actual number of copies of single issue published nearest to filing date: 7,143. C. Total paid and/or requested circulation. Average number of copies each issue during preceding 12 months: 7,375. Actual number of copies of single issue published nearest to filing date: 7,143. D. Free distribution by mail (complimentary and other free copies). Average number of copies each issue during preceding 12 months: 27. Actual number of copies of single issue published nearest to filing date: 26. E. Free distribution outside the mail (carriers or other means). Average number of copies of single issue during preceding 12 months: 24. Actual number of copies of single issue published nearest to filing date: 21. F. Total free distribution. Average number of copies each issue during preceding 12 months: 51 Actual number of copies of single issue published nearest to filing date: 47. G. Total distribution. Average number of copies each issue during preceding 12 months: 7,426. Actual number of copies of single issue published nearest to filing date: 7190. H. Copies not distributed. 1. Office use, left-over, unaccounted, spoiled after printing. Average number of copies each issue during preceding 12 months: 1,637. Actual number of copies of single issue published nearest to filing date: 3,260. 2. Return from news agents. Average number of copies each issue during preceding 12 months: 0. Actual number of copies of single issue published nearest to filing date: 0. I. Total (sum of G and H should equal net press shown in A). Average number of copies each issue during preceding 12 months: 9,063. Actual number of copies each issue published nearest filing date: 10,450. I certify that the statements made by me above are correct and complete. Gerald L. Durnell.

A Snap-on Truck
Every Living Ro

Or home office, or den, or wherever y
computer is.

We've made it easy for enthusiasts e
to find the Snap-on tools they would
have for their cars, boats, motorcycl
other toys. Log on to www.snapon.c
choose from more than 14,000 profe
quality tools, tool boxes, and test ins
the same tools that professionals ev
stake their reputations on every day
deliver them right to your door. Yo
will never be the same.

Snap-on.c

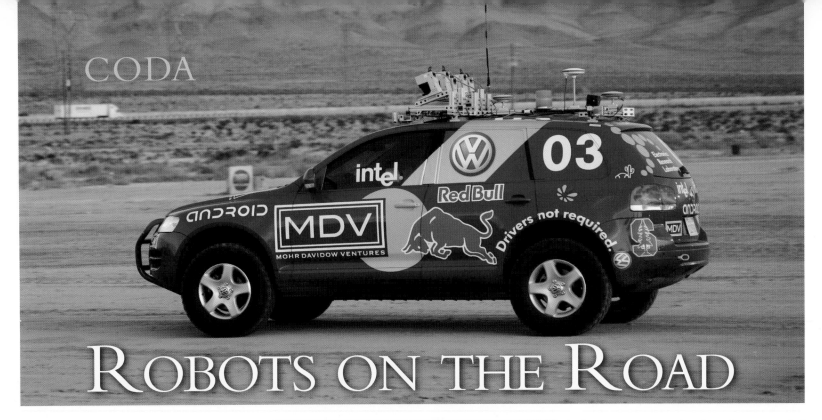

ROBOTS ON THE ROAD

Driverless vehicles have long been the subject of science fiction fantasy. Apparently the concept has recently joined the ranks of reality with an amazing winning performance from a modified VW Touareg named Stanley in a contest of technology and inventive skills in the blistering Mojave desert near Primm, Nevada. The design team was fundamentally comprised of the Volkswagen Electronics Laboratory, Stanford University and a number of commercial sponsors.

The event was the DARPA (Defense Advanced Research Project Agency) Grand Challenge and was held on October 10, 2005. Stanley's winning time was 6 hours, 53 minutes and 8 seconds, which was 11 minutes, 42 seconds faster than the second place finisher. The prize for first place was a lucrative $2 million. The first Grand Challenge ran in 2004 with a $1 million prize but no vehicle finished the inaugural race.

The 23 finalists in 2005 were selected from a field

> "A robot may not injure a human being or, through inaction, allow a human to come to harm."
>
> (The first of the three laws of robotics extracted from *I, Robot*, published 1950)
>
> —ISAAC ASIMOV—

of 195 teams through a series of qualifying races and ran a 132-mile course that led the vehicles over tough mountain roads, rocky mountain trails and dry lakebeds. The vehicles were limited to using only onboard sensors and navigational equipment with no human assistance.

The tools in the trunk included seven networked Pentium motherboards with 1.6 GHz processors fed from numerous sensors to give basic information as to what the car was doing. Simultaneously, laser detectors, stereo visual equipment and short-range 24-GHz radar systems were linked to a millimeter-accurate Global Positioning Satellite (GPS) system.

Stanley is built from a stock, diesel-powered Volkswagen Touareg R5 modified with full-body skid plates and a reinforced front bumper. Since its historic win, Stanley has been the star at the SEMA trade show in Las Vegas and on display at the Smithsonian in Washington, DC.

In keeping with the decades-old laws of robotics laid down decades ago in the prolific writings of Isaac Asimov, the underlying goal of the robotic exercise is to "not allow a human to come to harm." Reinforcing that 50-year-old admonition, Dr. Carlo Rummel, executive director of the Volkswagen of America's, Electronics Research Laboratory, noted: "The lessons we have learned. . . will ultimately benefit consumers as we apply this knowledge to make our vehicles safer, smarter and more exciting to drive." ◢◗

ML   3/07